APPALACHIAN HERITAGE

VOL. 44, NO. 3
SUMMER 2016

ESTABLISHED IN 1973

PUBLISHED QUARTERLY
by Berea College
CPO 2166
205 N. Main Street
Berea, KY, 40404

www.appalachianheritage.net

 Periodicals postage paid at Berea, Kentucky, and at additional mailing offices. ISSN# 03632318.

Electronic submissions only at www.appalachianheritage.net

Distributed by the University of North Carolina Press. Basic subscription price: $30/year for individuals, $60/year for institutions. For subscription requests and inquiries, visit the magazine's website, email uncpress_journals@unc.edu, or call 919.962.4201.

CONTENTS

INTERVIEW

CRAFT ESSAY

BOOK REVIEWS

COVER PHOTOGRAPH

EDITOR'S NOTE

JASON HOWARD

Dog days are upon us, those dreaded summer weeks of stifling temperatures and humidity that blanket the mountains and bottomlands. Some evenings, just before the gloaming descends, one can actually see the moisture hanging in the air, a ribbon wending just above the treeline. What helps to make these scorching days bearable for me are the tomatoes—a little late this year after such a parched summer.

They have come in all at once, so many that we are struggling to make use of them. Some have been canned. Others have been enjoyed right away, sliced to accompany a simple evening meal or placed on a sesame cracker with a dab of pesto and Welsh cheese for tea. Later this week, I'll be using the latest round to make *gazpacho*. They have become for me a symbol of hope this summer, the perfect antidote to this season of fear and anxiety in which we now find ourselves.

These are troubled times, with a presidential election that promises to be the most negative of many cycles, senseless shootings and attacks that have ravaged communities around the country and globe, and increasing amounts of vitriol and verbal assaults—fueled in part by social media—that have contributed to some of the worst divisions our country has ever seen. In such turbulent times, literature and the arts become even more important, helping us make sense of our tumultuous world and to appreciate the value of diversity and inclusivity. As President Kennedy once said, "When power corrupts, poetry cleanses."

What better cathedral than nature to serve as an antidote to such turmoil? A sunset "sending citrine light over the meadow canopy / Full summer crowns of maple and white oak," as in Jesse Graves's evocative poem "The Field at Rest." Or a wind that "worries the ridge" as "the pin oaks rattle and branches clack" in Jane Hicks's "Safety of Small Things."

What better way than thoughtful consideration to challenge ourselves? In his essay "Losing My Religion," Vic Sizemore does just that as he grapples with faith, reason, and doubt. Our interview with award-winning creative nonfiction author Sonja Livingston explores the connection between geography and identity. And Amanda Jo Runyon's craft essay "Robbing the Headlines" examines how real-life events can be used as inspiration for quality fiction.

What better strategy to conquer heat and fear than to confront them head on? In this issue's fiction, you'll encounter the story of a troubled home that unfolds poolside on a hot afternoon in Samantha Atkins's "Warble," a divorced couple whose ongoing lust and arguments are all bound up in a shared sorrow in Laura Leigh Morris's "Muddin," and a young widow and daughter who are submerged in a season of grief in Chelyen Davis's "Junebug."

As the summer begins to wane, I hope you'll carry this issue of *Appalachian Heritage* with you to the porch in the evenings or to read with your coffee in the cool of the mornings. I hope you'll allow the words of our contributors to both challenge and cleanse you. And I hope you'll savor the beauty and hope of homegrown tomatoes. ■

WARBLE

SAMANTHA ATKINS

It's a warble," said her Uncle Ted. "See em in squirrels sometimes." He drew on his cigarette and Leena watched its smoke spread out like fog around her mother's face.

It was a typical summer Saturday afternoon, she and her mother "baking," as her mother called it, in deck chairs around her aunt and uncle's in-ground pool. Leena and her mother had been staying there for two weeks while her father "packed his shit."

"Never heard of such a thing," replied her mother, also smoking, her exhale adding to the fog and enveloping Leena and the tiny kitten Leena held in her outstretched palm.

The kitten was sick. This was clear by the way everyone, including its brothers and sisters, avoided it in their crawling and tumbling around the pool deck. The kitten had a bulge in its neck like a tumor except this tumor had broken through its skin, creating a black circle filled with blood and flesh.

Leena had spotted the kittens under the deck land and coaxed them out. She had then carried the little sick-looking one up, inspecting its neck. She wondered if her mother would let her take one back to their house once her father was gone. Leena wasn't sure what had happened between her mother and father but she knew better than to ask too much. Her mother was the kind of person who liked you to mind your business. She was also the kind of person who thought adults were better off in the company of other adults than with children and that if a child, a child like Leena, had to be around, then it was best if she kept herself busy with something quiet.

The three of them, Leena, her mother, and her Uncle Ted, sat in a semi-circle, Leena holding the frail kitten and her mother and Uncle Ted lounging, stretched out in the sun next to one another. Something else beside tobacco smoke hung in the air around them as well, Leena thought, something like anger, that extra bit of heat filling the summer space.

"Something's in there?" Leena asked her uncle, holding up the kitten.

"Yep," said Uncle Ted, "Warble."

"Gross."

"Put it down," said Leena's mother, "you don't want to get whatever it is."

Leena nodded but did not set down the kitten. It was a tortoise shell kitten, mostly black with swirls and lines of brown, and its ears were pointed and larger than they seemed like they should be. Leena's teeth, she had been told, were also larger than they seemed like they should be. Her mother kept telling her not to worry—that she'd grow into them. She wondered if the kitten would die and never grow into its ears. Something behind her eyes swelled hot and stinging and she looked up to keep the tears from showing.

"Just let it die. It's gonna die anyway," said Uncle Ted as he tossed his glowing cigarette butt in the glass ashtray on the plastic deck table. Uncle Ted was like that with cats. It was a country thing, Leena's mother had told her. Uncle Ted was even more country than Leena's aunt Carrie, her mother's sister, and aunt Carrie was so country she knew how to skin a deer and debone a catfish and all kinds of other things that Leena could never imagine her mother doing.

Something behind her eyes swelled hot and stinging and she looked up to keep the tears from showing.

"Why would it die?" Leena asked, but Uncle Ted didn't hear her. He was already up and wobbling back into the kitchen. He had hurt his leg logging only a few weeks back and still hadn't regained all his strength.

"I'm going to kill it," said Leena.

"What?" replied her mother, "Leave it alone. You're not going to kill a kitten."

"Not the kitten, Mom, the warble. Go get me a tweezers."

Her mother rolled her eyes but stood up, tossed her own cigarette in the ash tray, and stepped barefoot across the deck toward Leena.

■ ■ ■

Her mother had been rolling her eyes less since they had started living with Aunt Carrie and Uncle Ted. Around her father, Leena's mother sighed, cursed, rolled her eyes, and pouted, though it wasn't always clear to Leena why she was so unhappy. She speculated that it wasn't really because her father "spent money like a teenager," but rather, that her mother was lonely. After all, none of her friends lasted very long around that kind of palpable unhappiness. Not to mention the drinking at night. Leena had overheard, for example, a nighttime conversation in which her mother had told an old friend all sorts of negative things about that friend's husband. He likely had another woman in Florida, she had said, and that's why he was insisting on traveling there alone for work. He also probably thought she was lazy for not holding a job because all men were like that—needing to find something or someone to blame.

■ ■ ■

Leena's mother took a last pull from her cigarette, tossed the still smoking butt, and said through the exhale, "Let me see it."

Leena held out the kitten, as gently as she could, as far from her body as possible. She didn't know what a warble was but anything living inside the neck of a baby couldn't be good. She didn't understand how there could be something alive in the lump unless it was in the shape of a perfect sphere. And how had it gotten there to begin with? She shuddered.

Leena's mother eyed the kitten but dared not touch it.

"What will you even grab with a tweezers? I can't see anything in there. Maybe it's further back in the neck."

"Will you get me some stuff to try at least?" asked Leena, knowing her mother to be a sucker for all things dead or dying. For years she had been dragging Leena to the nursing home down the street from their house to visit the "old people who don't have anyone in the world anymore." Leena had attended at least one funeral a month since as far back as she could remember and standing there thinking about it brought back that old, musty smell of baby's breath in bouquets.

Her mother shook her head and stood up slowly. She hadn't been injured but seeing as how she was already fifty-four, even though Leena was only twelve, she moved more slowly than other mothers.

■■■

With her mother gone, Leena was free to more closely examine the warble. Where was it? How could she make it come up to the hole? The kitten squirmed weakly in her hands. She set it down on the wood and, on all fours, crawled beside it, watching the bulge in its neck weigh it down. Were there multiple warbles? And what did they look like?

Leena thought back to the time her mother had forgotten to put out the trash before they left for the church weekend retreat. When they got back, Leena had gone to throw an empty pudding cup away when she saw them—hundreds of white, wriggling maggots, clinging to the sides of the can. She had gotten in trouble that day, she remembered, even though it wasn't her job to empty the trash. Still, when she had offered to help, she hadn't been allowed.

"Just go out and open the garage door. You need to mow," her mother had said, her face red as the plastic trash can and wet with sweat.

The poor kitten fell on its side as it tried to run.

"It's okay, buddy," Leena tried to tell him. "It's okay." But even as she said it, she felt herself tense in revulsion. What was it about parasites, she wondered, that made life seem so much more unbearable?

In quiet moments, like the one in which Leena sat, holding the suffering, squirming kitten, the truth of why her mother was so miserable surfaced and then resurfaced in Leena's mind. Her mother had never intended to have children and yet, here she was, saddled with Leena. How it happened was another one of those inquiries Leena knew better than to make aloud. Her mother and father had been married for ten years before conceiving her. Her mother had been forty-two and her father fifty-three. Had her mother relaxed with her birth control, thinking she was too old to get pregnant? Leena had learned about birth control in the special health class with just the girls. She knew about sex too, and lots of other things that she couldn't talk to her mother about.

■ ■ ■

Leena's mother returned from the house with a brown, square bottle of hydrogen peroxide, a half-used tube of Neosporin, a sandwich baggie full of cotton balls, and a pair of tweezers.

"Try this," she said, offering the tools to Leena.

Leena took the tweezers first. She poked the black and white mass inside the cat's neck. It seemed to recoil; the gaping skin around it opened and closed slightly.

"Maybe if I just clean it out..." said Leena, more to herself than to her mother.

"You two still messin' with that cat?" asked Uncle Ted, who had come back outside and began stretching out his leg, holding a can of Budweiser.

"She wants to try to save it," said Leena's mother, crossing her arms.

"It's gonna die out here anyway," said Uncle Ted. "You know how Carrie feels about them strays."

"She's got her mind made up," said her mother, "best just let her try to save it."

Leena poked the gaping hole where the parasitic creature writhed again and the kitten let out a cutting mew. Leena couldn't tell if the kitten was a boy or a girl, but she imagined it male. In the chance that she could save its life, she hoped it wouldn't have to be a girl so that it wouldn't have to someday mate with a male cat, which, she had read, had tiny spikes on their penises that would expand like needles once inside the female.

Leena realized, as she watched the bubbles, that the kitten had stopped fighting several minutes before. It lay limp in her hands, its tail stiff...

Leena switched tactics. She took the peroxide bottle, popped its white plastic top, and poured it onto the kitten's wound. White bubbles frothed around the circle.

"That's the blood burning off," said her mother, watching the kitten's wound expand and contract. Leena realized, as she watched the bubbles, that the kitten had stopped fighting several minutes before. It lay limp in her hands, its tail stiff—alive but terrified.

Uncle Ted began limping around the pool, using a long-handled pool skimmer to rake along its bottom. He held his beer in the opposite hand. "So how's school going?" he asked Leena. He always asked her broad questions like that. How was school? How was volleyball? How was that new boy she was going out with and what was his name again?

"Fine," she replied, still watching the kitten.

■ ■ ■

And school was fine, if she left out all the parts about her eating lunch by her locker alone because she had accidentally offended one of the girls in her friend group and gotten herself kicked out of it. School was fine if she also left out all the bits about how she was so over extended in the evenings with extracurricular stuff that she barely had enough time to do her homework. Softball, tap dancing, marching band, singing lessons—her mother wanted her to do it all. And school was fine if she remembered not to ask when she would see her dad again or what had happened.

Leena's mother seemed to smoke harder and harder on her cigarette as Uncle Ted skimmed the pool. It was amazing—the way she could have one endlessly glowing cigarette like that. Once, Leena had stolen a cigarette from her mother's purse late at night, taken it to the back porch, and nearly gagged on the inhale. It was one of many of Leena's secret attempts to understand her mother. She had wondered how it would feel to have something burning that close to her mouth and whether or not that burning could somehow tell her how she had come to exist.

She didn't only steal items from her mother's purse but Leena also listened when she knew she shouldn't. She pressed her ear against her bedroom door at night, listening hard, and that's how she had heard that she and her mother would be staying with her mother's sister Aunt Carrie. That's how she had heard her father saying "ridiculous" over and over and that's how she heard her mother crying after he had stormed out. She had laid on her bed after that, trying to fall back asleep, but then when she heard her mother leave too and peeked out the window to find both of their cars gone, Leena got up and snuck around the house.

She went into their bathroom and quietly, delicately, opened the cabinet doors and peeked around at the tiny bottles in order by size and the stacks of cotton rounds piled neatly on top of one another; her father was obsessed with tidiness. Leena was looking for anything, some indication of how she could know her mother so well and yet not at all. She unscrewed the tiny lids from the creams and gently dabbed her fingers in before smearing the stuff across her pimpled chin. She sprayed her mother's perfume into the air and breathed in deeply and quickly, thinking that it might hold some key—might awaken some infant memory.

■ ■ ■

The tortoise-shell kitten twitched in her hands. "Whoa!" said Leena, "Look—Oh my God."

"Language," said Uncle Ted.

The warble had begun to move and appeared to be sticking out of the cat's neck slightly so that Leena could see that the circle that looked like blood and flesh was not the kitten's neck but rather the mouth of the parasite.

"That's its mouth!" she almost yelled.

"Let me see," said her mother, crowding in beside her. "Oh that's disgusting."

"I'm tellin' you, you should leave it alone. Half the time them warbles just crawl out and leave anyway," added Uncle Ted, walking around the pool slowly to join the spectacle.

Leena grabbed the tweezers from the deck floor and, quicker than she thought herself capable, grasped the warble by the lip of its hideous mouth.

"Fuck," she whispered, her heart swelling, her lungs holding her back from breath.

"This how you let your daughter talk?" Uncle Ted asked Leena's mother.

"My daughter talks how she wants to. She works hard—she can say what she likes."

This was a sentiment Leena's mother had never before expressed and in the split second Leena allowed herself to think of anything aside from the wriggling creature she, she considered it. Why was her mother talking to Uncle Ted like that? They usually got along.

"Got it!" Leena pulled slowly but steadily and the black, ringed worm slid from the noiseless kitten and hung in the air from the tweezers.

"I can't believe you did it," said Leena's mother, extinguishing her cigarette on the deck.

"Get rid of it," said Uncle Ted.

"No," said Leena, "go grab me a plastic baggie, somebody. I want to save it. I want to look it up and like, cut it open or something."

Uncle Ted shook his head and took one last swig from his beer can before crunching it in his fist and turning to go back inside.

"You're a little *different* aren't you?" he asked Leena without a hint of humor.

"I'll get you the bag," said her mother. "Ooh or even better—maybe we should leave it for Aunt Carrie in a pickle jar. It would scare the shit out of her."

"You leave that thing anywhere in my house and you know what'll happen to it," said Uncle Ted.

Leena watched the warble writhe, putting her eyes right up to it. Its black and silver body contracted into a ball and then expanded again to be at least four inches long. How could it have even fit inside the kitten? Leena's mother stepped silently in her bare feet to the back door that led into the kitchen and Uncle Ted turned and tromped directly behind her, leaving Leena alone, again.

Leena was used to being alone, even when her parents were in the house with her. Even without brothers and sisters, she entertained herself, writing stories in her head with her dolls and hanging upside down on the couch, imagining being able to walk on the ceilings. Her mother always said that she had felt the same way as a kid, completely independent, until Aunt Carrie was born anyway.

Aunt Carrie was twelve years younger than Leena's mother and nothing like her. Aunt Carrie was religious for one thing, going to the Wesleyan church every Sunday morning and then again Wednesday evenings for Bible studies. Leena's mother said every preacher she had ever met was a sexist sonofabitch and that she'd rather sleep in on the weekends. Aunt Carrie was shorter than Leena's mother, and a little bit rounder as well. She dressed more conservatively and never drank beer. She'd heard her mother say, more than once, that Aunt Carrie had come into the world "charmed" and that she would leave it the same way, getting everything she wanted in between.

Leena released the kitten who immediately began mewing and stumbling around the deck. She reached for the bottle of peroxide and poured it, perhaps too liberally, into the cat's wound. It bubbled only slightly this time and upon closer inspection, Leena saw that the hole was mostly clean on the inside. It was flesh-colored and cavernous and it seemed not to bother the kitten at all.

From the kitchen Leena heard the thud of what might have been a drawer slamming shut and then a clanging as though something had knocked into her aunt's pots hanging from the ceiling.

"Mom?" she yelled.

The warble was growing tired at the end of the tweezers, dancing less and less, while the kitten was energized, hopping from wooden slat to wooden slat on the deck's floor, chasing a fly.

It felt as though five minutes had passed since Leena had been left on the deck. She had been sitting in the heat so long that the excitement of her accomplishment had gone from feeling like an explosion to something more akin to a pile of low burning embers. Her arm grew tired from holding the warble and she feared for what might happen were the kitten to trip into the swimming pool. The warble might get lost in the struggle were she to have to jump in for the kitten. And could one perform CPR on a kitten the way that she had been taught to perform it on an adult in health class?

Leena stood up and tiptoed to the tiny window that hung right above the kitchen sink. She wasn't sure why she was tiptoeing but it seemed like the best way to move at that moment. Her fingers squeezed the tweezers tightly and since her hand was nearly numb, she clasped it with the other hand to keep the worm from slipping away.

It was luck that she had done this, use both hands to hold the tweezers, because had she been only using one, she would've surely dropped the warble at what she saw. Her mother, pressed against the refrigerator, holding a sandwich

Leena stood up and tiptoed to the tiny window that hung right above the kitchen sink. She wasn't sure why she was tiptoeing but it seemed like the best way to move at the moment.

baggie out to the side while Uncle Ted—her Uncle!—leaned against her, working his hand under her bikini cover up. Her mother's eyes were closed and her face scrunched as though ready to yell at someone. Leena couldn't see her uncle's face, just the scruffy, short hair on the back of his neck and the V-shaped stain of sweat on his T-shirt.

She felt something kick inside her lower abdomen and heat spread down her legs and up to her cheeks all at once. She was so ashamed to feel it that it was almost painful, that heat. What was her mother thinking? Or was it all Uncle Ted? Did her mother need her help? She stepped back, almost tripping and falling on the kitten behind her.

Suddenly everything was too hot—the bottoms of her feet on the deck wood, the sweat around her temples, the tweezers in her hand. The tweezers were especially hot, as though her aunt were inside them, squeezing tightly the warble against the sight of Leena's mother against the fridge.

Leena knew what shock felt like. She had felt it the day last summer when her grandfather had passed away. Uncle Ted had been there too—she just remembered. It was during a softball game and Leena had been playing well for once. Her mother was in the stands holding a can of Diet Coke between her knees and Uncle Ted had been sitting beside her. How many games had he come to? And why hadn't Leena ever noticed?

That day she had stepped out of the dugout and her mother had told her that her grandfather had passed away from a heart attack. The shock was like time slowing down. It was like the chanting of her teammates growing duller and softer, so soft she couldn't make out what they were saying. It was like the cars driving past weren't really moving anymore.

"Why aren't I crying?" she had asked her mother.

"You're in shock," her mother had said, and then they had walked to the car and driven to her grandfather's house to be with the rest of the family.

That was what she felt like now, a year older but still capable of stopping time and hearing less. The warble stopped moved. The kitten froze, perched on the edge of the pool. The buzzing of the flies and mosquitoes around her face fell silent. Her mother pushed open the kitchen door with her hip and, still carrying the plastic baggie, walked to Leena, smiling.

"I changed my mind," Leena blurted. "I don't want to save it."

"Good," said her mother, "no need to save such a nasty thing."

"Let's throw it in the woods," said Leena, "or drown it in the pool."

"No," said her mother, "what if another creature comes along and tries to eat it? It might get infected too."

Leena stared at her mother's teeth, the top row so perfectly aligned and square that they seemed like a movie star's despite the staining of the tar around their edges.

"Let's burn it then," said Leena.

"Yeah," her mother agreed. "Let's burn it."

Leena's mother reached inside the screened-in porch and grabbed a roll of paper towel from an end table with a seashell carved on the side. She then scooped up the kitten with her empty hand and cradled it against her bare stomach. Leena found herself looking away from her mother over and over as each glimpse of her red and black bikini brought back the sight of Uncle Ted against her. She would not look at her mother. She would not look at Uncle Ted. And in not looking, she would forget what she'd seen. What she had, perhaps, always seen. Uncle Ted at her birthday parties without Aunt Carrie. Uncle Ted bringing over that kerosene heater when the electricity had gone out. No—Leena would not look at her mother's bikini.

Carrying the still-squirming warble in her aunt's tweezers, Leena followed her mother down the deck steps and across the backyard to a spot with a squat, fat tree stump. She watched her mother, still barefoot, step delicately up to the trunk and place paper towel upon paper towel on it as though creating a bed for a doll. The kitten struggled against her and caught her skin in its claw, causing her to yelp and drop it on the grass.

"Be careful," yelled Leena, but the kitten was fine. It rolled in the grass and then hopped after a cricket as though nothing had happened at all.

"Put it on there," said her mother, pointing to the stump.

Leena held the baggie upside down and shook it so that the fat, black body of the warble plopped out onto the paper towel. Her mother held her cigarette lighter out to Leena.

"You do it," she said, "I'm not getting close to that thing."

Leena took the lighter and adjusted it in her hand so she was holding it correctly. She walked up to the tree stump, but instead of trying to light the paper towel on fire, she knelt down and put her face close to the warble. It rolled and squirmed like a baby does, blind. Why didn't she want to save its life like she had the kitten? It was just as helpless. Yet there was something about it—she wondered again what it would look like on the inside.

"Hurry up and do it," said her mother, "that thing's grossing me out."

Leena grabbed a thin stick off the ground and poked into the warble. It squirmed and fought, but she pushed through anyway. Blood oozed from the puncture wound. Kitten blood.

"Disgusting," said her mother, "I'm not gonna watch this."

She stepped, carefully in her bare feet, back to the deck steps.

Leena saw in a flash how the rest of the night would go. Aunt Carrie coming home, Uncle Ted watching TV, her mother working a Sudoku puzzle outside until the sun went down. It would be a good night for her aunt and for her uncle and for her mother and for the kitten. And she would let them have that.

After two failed attempts, Leena finally got the lighter to strike a flame. She held it close to the warble, directly on the paper towel. After a few seconds, the paper towel caught fire and the flames slowly but surely crawled to meet the warble, whose body rolled around furiously but, with the stick still through it, had no where to go.

When it was over, when the paper towels were just black ashes on the stump and the kitten had run back to its family under the deck, Leena wiggled the stick around uncovering the warble's body. It hadn't burned too much itself, but either the smoke or the stick had killed it and it had shrunk with its death so that with it lying there like that, all stretched out and in the open, it looked almost like a charred cigarette butt and she knew why it was she hadn't saved it in the end. ■

BARN SWALLOWS

They made a sound like wind
coming to life, ignition that always
startled me, though I knew
the swallows would be sleeping there.
They hid where I wanted to hide,
up in the rafters, up above the loft,
above the broken tobacco sticks,
unstrung bales of hay, cracked tires,
barbed edges of nails, staples, and wire.

The barn gave work and shelter
from work, and late in the fall,
when leaves began to gather up
their transient colors and scatter
into hidden corners to crumble,
cracks in the barn walls whistled
and chimed, made soft music,
like rows of flutes and violins
played by an orchestra of ghosts.

I came there to play child-games
among the throwaway parts,
build obstacle courses for bright
metal cars to race through.
I came there to disappear,
become a vessel for any message
the birds wanted to deliver,
wings fluttering along my spine,
voices like tiny bells in my ears.

JESSE GRAVES

EDITH

My job was to pour the mold
for the hard porcelain crowns
that sat on telephone poles.
I rode the bus to the plant,
even when they called it
"the scab bus." I wasn't proud
to take someone else's job.
My husband was sick in bed,
and I needed the money.
I was willing to work hard
when others wouldn't do it.
I worked until the day
my brother needed me back
home, and I went to where
I could do some good, and kept
him until he died one night.
How much did I choose of life?
How many days did I wish
for what I saw others waste?
I could say I had no time
to think of such things, but why
would I want to lie about
anything now, near the end?
I want to say what happened,
to tell the truth about all
I went without, all I needed
and never got, though I know
no one listened then, and no
one is likely to listen now.

JESSE GRAVES

THE FIELD AT REST

Across a field no one is watching right now,
The sun sets through high orange-streaked clouds,
Sending citrine light over the meadow canopy,
Full summer crowns of maple and white oak,
Tulip poplar, shagbark, and layers of scrub pine.
Cows keep the grass cropped, but not too short,
Far from the pond, and steeper than other grazing.
Deer nibble at the edges, and bed down there
Some nights, where I have startled them in groups
At sunset, sending their hooves skittering away.
My father has buried cows in the far corner,
One time not deep enough, and coyotes scattered
Bones out in the open and far into the woods.
At this hour, the cows will have gathered closer
To the barn, and nothing much will be moving,
Just the eyes, always scanning from the edges,
Loping along just under cover of shadows.
My father is home nursing the many illnesses
Of his age, maybe on the porch with his dog,
Maybe still about feeding chickens and ducks.
My mother will be cleaning the dinner dishes,
Also stepping out to the porch to divide
Scraps between the cats and yard dogs.
Later I will call them on the phone,
Ask about the animals, their medicines,
Any trips the day might have brought.
But the field, right now, I know it's empty,
I know I could walk through the late light

Across this untraveled back trail,
Almost into another time, stepping quicker
Than the quick-closing shadows.

JESSE GRAVES

LOSING MY RELIGION

VIC SIZEMORE

I grew up in a strict fundamentalist Baptist home beside a mud-brown river in Elkview, West Virginia. From the door of my house to the front doors of the Baptist church, where my dad preached for thirty-eight years, was a walk of about fifty steps. From the back of the house, once you stepped out of the yard you were standing before the twin metal doors of the pole barn that served as the church gymnasium. Inside were two sets of basketball hoops on padded poles; the floor markings were not those of a basketball court however, but of two AWANA circles. AWANA is a club where children have team competitions on the circle and learn arts and crafts, but that is just a way to get the kids in. The real purpose of AWANA is to make kids memorize Bible verses and imbibe the Absolute Truth they contain.

I will give you the short version of what I grew up learning was Absolute Truth: God created the world fully formed, sometime between six- and ten-thousand years ago. Eve sinned first, and then Adam with her, bringing death and suffering to all earthly creatures, and eternal hellfire to humans after death. God established different governments, or dispensations, for dealing with people and giving them a way to get to heaven and avoid hell; we are in the age of grace, which means you are saved from hell by asking Jesus to come into your heart, save you, and be your personal Lord and Savior—there is no other way. All these claims are true because the Bible says they are true and the Bible is the inerrant, infallible Word of God; the Bible is the infallible Word of God because it is written in the Bible. Finally, if you question any of these articles of faith you are at best backsliding, and at worst, not saved and dangling dangerously over eternal hellfire.

This was the constant driving message of my pastor father, and the guiding principles of my mother's work as a keeper at home. I came to ignore it as best I could—which you had to do to keep from becoming a basket case thinking of all those millions of people dying and tumbling into eternal suffering, all because you had not gotten to them in time with the Good News of Jesus. When I was in high school, my chief interests were playing soccer and writing bad poetry to a long series of girls I loved with all the passion in my youthful heart. I went to church, as they say, every time the doors were open. The soccer team and the Elkview Baptist Church youth group were my circles.

The youth group was vibrant and growing at this time—a cult of personality, as those kinds of bursts always are, though parents speak of how the Lord is working or the Spirit is moving among the kids. The personality in EBC's youth group at this time was Joe.

Joe was one of those youth pastors who seemed to have a sure calling, the kind of guy people called *on fire for the Lord.* He preached fearlessly, with the zeal of a prophet; unlike others who believed they had the gift of prophecy, Joe did not see it as an excuse to be a loud and judgmental asshole. He was open and honest, transparent about his struggles. It drew us kids to him. He and his wife opened their home to us, were endlessly patient with the teenage noise, hormones, strife.

Joe's Sunday school classroom was packed. He led emotionally charged prayer meetings and revival gatherings, full of crying and repentance. He had a beard and crazy hair, and eyes as wild as John Brown raiding Harper's Ferry.

In 1983, an anti-rock and roll wave that swept through the group after they went downtown to a Marty Tingelhoff crusade where the evils of rock 'n roll music were presented along with musical demonstrations. Tingelhoff played The Eagles and Led Zeppelin and ELO backwards—and, yes, Queen's "Another One Bites the Dust"—so that the kids could hear the satanic back-masked messages. After that, Joe instructed us to bring all our secular cassettes to his house. On his front driveway, on the mountainside across 119 from EBC, perched up on the mountainside, Joe had a wheelbarrow on his front drive, where we pitched their devil music and hosed it down with lighter fluid. We stood in a circle as the black smoke twisted from the melting plastic and coated our nostrils and throats with the taste of chemical poison. Boys took turns squirting lighter fluid to make flare-ups.

Weak to the power of music though, I caved to temptation. My friend Danny tossed in his Pink Floyd *The Wall* cassette and it fell to the edge and rested there intact. Pink Floyd was my favorite band, and I felt horrible guilt, but I slid it into my pocket when no one was looking. The case was a little melted, but the tape played fine.

Around the burning rock 'n roll, we sang songs, and took turns praying. We sang "It Only Takes a Spark," one from Joe's youth, among other songs. Attempted by a different youth pastor, this could have been a disaster of uncool adult intrusion. Joe had an alternative though, one that made the adults uneasy, which heightened the appeal. He had Christian rock 'n roll.

He loaded the youth group up and took us to a Petra concert down in Charleston—"God Gave Rock and Roll To You" Petra—before ersatz rock 'n roll with sappy Christian

He led emotionally charged prayer meetings and revival gatherings, full of crying and repentance. He had a beard and crazy hair, and eyes as wild as John Brown raiding Harper's Ferry.

lyrics was called Contemporary Christian Music—offering us an alternative to secular rock 'n roll.

Joe's approval of rock music—Christian or not, the beat itself was used in Africa to call up evil spirits, missionaries knew—was a problem. It got the parents watching him. His leaving the youth group seemed inevitable after the fact, but it was a shock when it happened.

What got Joe into real trouble with the church leadership was the doctrine of biblical inerrancy. In front of the youth group, Joe talked of his intense study of scripture, and puzzled over how the Bible could possibly be inerrant—

but then backed off and said of course it was. He asked honest questions, and though he always came to acceptable conclusions in front of the class, we could all see he wasn't comfortable with them.

Because he was unpredictable behind the lectern, inconsistent, doctrinally shaky, the church leadership shunned Joe. I never found out if he was asked to step down, or if he quit, but his leaving was abrupt. Disgusted that asking honest questions could get you ostracized, I checked out of the youth group.

■ ■ ■

After high school, I worked at UPS and did a year at West Virginia State, and then capitulated to my parents' wishes and enrolled at Liberty University in Lynchburg, Virginia. I chafed under the rules, neglected my studies, played club soccer and lacrosse, and slipped off campus to drink beer with friends.

William Perry's well-known stages of growth maps the intellectual and ethical development of a college student from dualism through multiplicity and relativism to a mature and informed commitment. The first stage, dualism, is characterized by either/or, black/white thinking and the appeal to authority for validation of one's beliefs. The problem with Liberty, as with all fundamentalist colleges, is that just when young people need developmentally to move through these stages, they find themselves in an institution whose goal is to solidify them in dualism, keep them in the moral universe of childhood. I had to get out.

After spring semester of 1986, I enlisted in the Marine Corps Reserves. Upon return from boot camp, I enrolled, with my younger brother Vaughn, at Marshall University, and moved to the southwestern edge of West Virginia where it converges with Ohio and Kentucky along the Ohio River. I did not do well in my classes here either, but I did do a lot of reading. In Joseph Campbell's *The Hero with a Thousand Faces*, for example, I read of Osiris, the dying and resurrecting god who was the hope of eternal life for Egyptians, how sarcophagi have his face on them because people wanted to literally put off themselves and put on Osiris. The god-man who had beat death would be their face, so they could get safely through the land of the dead. I thought as I read of Paul's admonitions in Romans and Galatians to clothe yourself in Christ. I also read of Isis, who was impregnated miraculously as she never found Osiris's penis. She gave birth to a god after this nonsexual impregnation. Echoes of Mary, mother of Jesus.

In my college apartment in Huntington, West Virginia, surrounded by the stink of dirty dishes and my roommate Curt's neglected pit bull, I struggled with the angst these stories brewed inside me. That fall semester, my brother Curt and I huddled around a gas wall heater while snowflakes blew through gaps between the windowpanes. I read *Paradise Lost* for my Milton class. I read *Areopagitica*.

I still have my Milton textbook, *Complete Poems and Major Prose*, from that class. Looking back through it, I see that the young me highlighted *and* underlined the passage in which the sad friends of Truth, "imitating the careful search that Isis made for the mangled body of Osiris," cast about looking for the Truth that has been "hewed…into a thousand pieces, and scattered…to the four winds."

I read the *Epic of Gilgamesh* with its flood story, which predates Moses by hundreds of years, and contains the story of Utnapishtim, the ur-Noah. Flood stories abound in world mythology, but the Bible's account is so strikingly similar to the story of Utnapishtim. In Genesis, the reason God destroys humanity is that the "wickedness of man was great on the earth, and every imagination of his heart was only evil continually." In a number of translations of the *Gilgamesh* version, the gods are disturbed by humanity's noise. The same reason Grendel lopes out of the moors to wreak havoc on the drunken thanes at Heorot. Excessive noise. What is it about making too much noise that deserves supernatural retribution, whether it comes from gods or devils? You could imagine that whenever large groups of humans are making enough noise to wake up the gods, they are having a very good time or a very bad time, a bacchanal or a war. Excess then. Too much of something.

Gilgamesh also has a serpent—the common enemy and bringer of death in ancient Mesopotamian literature—who slithers up and makes off with the hero's one shot at eternal life. Gilgamesh's wild-man sidekick Enkidu is created by a goddess when she scoops up clay from the ground, forms it

You could imagine that whenever large groups of humans are making enough noise to wake up the gods, they are having a very good time or a very bad time, a bacchanal or a war.

into the shape of a man, and breathes life into him—exactly as God later creates Adam in the Bible. New discoveries bloomed before me with every new passage. The world of ancient mythology was chock-full of uncanny parallels to stories I had grown up hearing were the absolute, literal, and authoritative versions of history.

To a child of fundamentalism, this was more than a little disorienting, but those parallels were just the beginning of my trouble. Modern science, I already knew from the evolution battle, had chucked all these competing truth claims into the same bin labeled *the best we could do before we knew better.*

The scientific evidence has long been more than enough to justify abandoning a literal reading of the early chapters of Genesis. More recent genetic research has rendered it all but unavoidable. Non-fundamentalist Christians accept it. On the Christian *BioLogos Forum* blog "Ham on Nye: Our Take," Fellow of Biology Dennis Venema writes that if young-earth creationism is true, then "why do humans, as placental mammals, have the defective, fragmentary remains of [a] gene for making egg yolk in our genome exactly where one would predict it to be based on examining the genomes of egg-laying organisms?" He continues, "Why is it that we share many mutations in this defective gene with other placental mammals, to say nothing of the many other defective genes with the same pattern of shared mutations?"

The present textbook war in the American South notwithstanding, creationism is headed for the dustbins of history, to take its place alongside the geocentric universe, and a literal hell in the center of the earth, and those countless other beliefs that I grew up learning were inviolable and essential to true faith.

Getting out of Elkview, and away from Liberty University, was for me like being lifted from a small creek and thrown into the middle of the sea. The mad stormy swirl of ideas was both terrifying and exhilarating. In contrast, the Pre-Millennial Dispensational theology of my childhood was one calcified piece, each point taught with the same absolute certainty as every other. I began to notice oddities in this theological landscape. Stones seemed fake, held in place unnaturally—the literal twenty-four hour, six-day creation six thousand years ago say; or the doctrine of verbal, plenary biblical inspiration and its subsequent inerrancy—and I started to kick at those stones.

I finally kicked away a stone—decided I could not believe in a literal talking snake causing all the world's woes any more than I could believe in a literal, historical Pandora. That one stone fell away. Then the belief in biblical inerrancy had to go, and the collapse began. The ground crumbled from beneath me in outward circles like ripples on water. Everything my life was built on fell away until I was floating, totally unmoored, casting about among the twisting and drifting fragments of my childhood faith, trying to cobble something together that I could live with—all the while trying to evade the come-back-to-Jesus talks dad's preacher friends from Huntington were dropping in to spring on me.

This realization came with real trepidation. Had I discovered that everything my entire world was built on was a lie? Could I voice my opinions and questions at home? Disappoint everyone I knew? Become a shunned outsider? Bring the wrath of an angry God down on my head? Would I break my parents' hearts, make them fear for my eternal soul? What about my eternal soul? Did I even have one? What if I did and hell was real after all?

It is no wonder the tale of the bumpkin going off to college and becoming an angry atheist is a cliché—you have to talk yourself up to leaving, arm yourself against the judgments of your family and community. It is no wonder either that so many give up, declare themselves agnostic, and choose to think no more about it but rather turn their attention to actually living in this world.

When T. H. Huxley coined the word agnostic, he explained, "It is wrong for a man to say he is certain of the objective truth of a proposition unless he can produce evidence which logically justifies that certainty." To Huxley, metaphysical, religious, spiritual claims are of no use. People I knew who called themselves agnostic said something like, "No one knows for certain, so why waste any more time and energy on it?" What can anyone say definitively about the truth of any religion? About God?

■ ■ ■

I sat on the day bed in my den on Sunday, March 11, 2012, and read an article in the *New York Times* obituaries. I don't normally read the obits, but they had included an article about William Hamilton, the man at the center of the "Death of God" controversy back in April of 1966. I remembered hearing about it as a child. One evangelist mentioned it in chapel service at Elk Valley Christian School. He said sneeringly that these death-of-god people believed God had become so heartbroken by the evil of humanity that he'd given up hope, rolled over and died.

Hamilton's ideas have nothing to do with the actual death of a divine being. "The 'death of God' is a metaphor," he told *The Oregonian* in 2007. "We needed to redefine Christianity as a possibility without the presence of God." This was not nearly as radical as it sounded, at least not to academic theologians, who had been dealing with this at the very least since Nietzsche.

When Nietzsche trumpeted the death of God, he was not announcing the actual death of any god, but of the "metaphysical logos," as Martin Heidegger terms it in his book, *Nietzsche*. He was declaring an end to any overarching meaning, any whole and entire explanation for why we are here and what our purpose is. Nietzsche's point is that God never existed in the first place; what died was the illusion that we can explain our existence in any meaningful way.

Reading about Hamilton and Nietzsche, I thought of the *mythos* and *logos* of the Ancient Greeks, the principles governing their whole cosmos and the basis for all human reason and understanding—and the *logos* of Judaism, the word of God, the way in which He communicated with them, and, moreover a creative power in its own right. These are the things Nietzsche is declaring obsolete in the modern world. Hamilton's "death of God" is an attempt to find, in the skeptical light of the modern world, a livable religion stripped of this particular meaning, stripped of any divine presence.

A livable religion stripped of divine presence appears to what Alain de Botton is proposing in his book, *Religion for Atheists*. In an interview on Wisconsin Public Radio, de Botton spoke admiringly of religion, of all the human needs it meets, and said his hope is that atheists can co-opt what is good about it without bringing along its ancient and disproven superstitions.

Next interviewed on the same show was Adam Frank, author of *The Constant Fire*. Frank went a step further, saying that not believing in God does not mean he cannot believe in some kind of "spiritual reality," or at least leave open the possibility. He bases this on personal anecdotal evidence: he has had his own epiphanies, and cannot bring himself to admit they are no more than reactions firing off inside his wet brain. Maybe you say these are soft atheists, not good examples, not real like the so-called New Atheists who take a harder line.

What about the New Atheists? Listen to how they revere science and reason. Go to the Symphony of Science website and watch the "Wave of Reason" video. Richard Dawkins speaks of the "new wave of reason, where superstition had a firm hold," his voice auto-tuned to sound like singing. Planetary scientist Carolyn Porco says, "The same spiritual fulfillment that people find in religion can be found in science by coming to know, if you will, the mind of God," as the praise and worship music plays.

■ ■ ■

I was riding with my daughter Grace in the back of a friend's car, heading home from a music festival. My wife was up front with our friend Virginia, who is weird and fun and loves everything quirky and new. Virginia put on the latest They Might Be Giants CD for children called *Here Comes Science*. The sing-along melodies and catchy hooks were just what you would expect from the nerd rockers.

Grace liked it immediately. The songs were little lessons about things like the scientific method ("If there's a question bothering your brain / that you think you know how to explain / You need a test / Yeah, think up a test."), and what various scientists do ("I Am a Paleontologist").

Then the song "Science Is Real" came on. They sang that they "like the stories about angels, unicorns and elves," but, "when I'm seeking knowledge, either simple or abstract, the facts are with science." They set up Science against religion (and the arts incidentally) as having a surer claim on reality, on "the facts."

My friend was a product of a conservative Christian home, just as I was—I remember sitting in Sunday school as a child, swinging my feet to the rhythm and belting out, "I'm no kin to the monkey / The monkey's no kin to me / I don't know about your grandpa / but mine didn't swing from a tree"—and we both chuckled a little as They Might Be Giants poked fun at some of the beliefs we had left behind.

Then I noticed that at the end of the song, They Might Be Giants switched from "the facts are with science" to "the truth is with science." With this, they went from offering science as a paradigm for trying to understand reality to holding up Science as reality itself.

The song was staking a metaphysical claim.

It is understandable, but their problem is this: the metaphysical claim made in "Science Is Real" is a claim that cannot be proven by the method they admonish young listeners to use. They sing, "If somebody says they've figured it out / And they're leaving room for doubt / Come up with a test." But "science is real" is a claim that lies outside the bounds of any empirical test, which is the price of admission into Science; using their own rules, they cannot verify their most basic truth claim.

I thought about Gödel's incompleteness theorem: every system is either incomplete (there are true statements that cannot be contained within it) or it has internal inconsistencies or paradoxes (there are coexisting claims that cannot simultaneously be true). *Antinomy* is the more precise word: assertions that negate one another, and yet are still both held to be equally true. Though Gödel is referring to formal mathematical systems, it is worth applying this to religious and philosophical systems because none that claims universality is without paradox.

There is, for example, for Christians the problem of evil: how, in a world where evil exists, can there be a creator God who is both all good and all-powerful? To believe in an omnipotent and omniscient God in a world where evil does not just exist but flourishes, is to cling to paradox. In *The*

Our paradoxes are the load-bearing points, the capstones that hold our structures together. Here are the deep places of mystery.

Bhagavad-Gita, the warrior Arjuna despairs that if he does his duty and kills his kin in battle he will bring evil upon himself. He asks Krishna "how can we know happiness," which is his heart's desire. Krishna tells him he must do his duty, but "relinquish attachment." He instructs Arjuna that he can achieve his desire for happiness, "when he gives up desires in his mind, is content with the self within himself." When Arjuna can act without desire, when for him "suffering and joy are equal" his actions will not affect his happiness. You want your heart's desire, Arjuna? Give up desire, do your duty as a warrior, and you will find it.

Likewise, absolute believers in Science make a claim that cannot be subjected to their own empirical method. It is beyond the realms of science, is a paradoxical truth claim and must be accepted on faith.

In these crazy times when legitimate science is rejected on religious grounds, I want to be clear: I do not advocate rejecting the sure findings of science. However, we live with mystery, all of us, and we believe paradoxes—not minor glitches, easily overlooked, but at the place where something major is at stake. Our paradoxes are the load-bearing points, the capstones that hold our structures together. Here are the deep places of mystery.

Does it come down to which paradox, which mystery, you can abide? Whether we do it with religion or reason or science, aren't we all trying to sate what Albert Camus calls "an appetite for the absolute and for unity"? Is Dostoevsky's Grand Inquisitor right when he says, there is "nothing a free [person] is so anxious to do as to find something to worship"?

■ ■ ■

Several months ago, I heard Marilynne Robinson in discussion with Marcelo Gleiser on the radio show *On Being with Krista Tippett*. Robinson says that, "contemporary science" is making discoveries "as profound as Galileo ever was, or Copernicus." She marvels at "the idea that we can know things that absolutely revolutionize previous models of the universe we inhabit." This is equally true if we are looking out at the vast universe, or in at the tiniest structures we have found so far.

Gleiser agrees, "Everything is in transformation at all times." History is a series of rethinking our myths in light of new discoveries. The enemy is not knowledge. Knowledge, like every other living thing, shifts and evolves. In order to live gracefully with it, we must remain supple and adroit. Gleiser stresses that this does not mean being "pious toward science" because "when you adopt the idea that there is only one way of knowing a thing, then you are robbing humanity of its value."

Robinson goes on to say these creation myths "anticipate modern cosmology." They are "the expression of the intuition of cosmology among ancient people." Gleiser agrees: "All the scientific models, the theories that cosmologists used to explain the universe reproduced mythic ideas. There was a universe that was cyclical, like the dancing of Shiva…the Big Bang was prefigured by creation myths." For me, it is exhilarating to think of the mythology I learned as a child in these terms. All those stories that were once dead relics come roaring back to life.

■■■

Since the onset of social media, I have reconnected with friends who knew me back when I was a Baptist. They ask me where I stand vis-à-vis the old time religion. And I tell them. In our tradition there are those who backslide, those who were once on fire for the Lord and have fallen away. Then there are those, like me, who have left The Faith.

According to Hebrews 11:1, "faith is the substance of things hoped for, the evidence of things not seen." The evidence of things not seen is faith in those unseen things. This appears to be some very clumsy circular reasoning, and that can be a little frustrating, especially when it demands of you that you disregard anything that contradicts or even questions it.

Miguel de Unamuno claims that the longing for immortality in the human soul is enough to justify belief in immortality. Faith itself is evidence that the unseen object of that faith is substantial. Is that all we get? Would it be enough?

Apparently it is not enough for most people. The absolute claims of my childhood faith on the other hand, offer certainty and comfort in a chaotic and scary world. Even for those who know that the fundamentalists' claims of historical and scientific accuracy are false, the gravity of that world is strong. It took me years of effort to escape its pull, to break free of its orbit.

My youth pastor Joe, who was shunned for questioning biblical inerrancy, is one of the people I reconnected with on social media. He has been pulled back into the world of fundamentalism, is once again on fire for the Lord. He is once again proclaiming the absolute truth of this faith, a truth he knows, as preachers from my childhood often said from the pulpit, "beyond the shadow of a doubt."

There was a time when I felt I had to have all the answers, had to know beyond the shadow of a doubt. No more. I think of a character in Don Delillo's novel *Falling Man*. In the wake of the attacks of 9/11, she thinks about all the variations of belief in the world and decides she is "free to think and doubt and believe simultaneously." This sounds fair and honest to me.

That does not mean I call myself agnostic. It is true, when my friends ask, I say *I don't know*, but it isn't quite that simple. I asked my friend Amy, who is a professor of classics, what she would call someone who doesn't know but hopes to someday find out. She suggested *proupomenognostic*, explaining that *upomeno* means await, endure, abide. *Proupomenognostic* sounds good. I await a time when I will know that knowing is possible, even if it is always a knowing that thrives somehow, paradoxically, in the midst of doubt, hunger, longing. ■

AGENT OF PROVIDENCE

Roma Downey glows on the television screen,
her angel touch dispensed, the plot line closed.
I have muted the sound as my mother drifts toward sleep.
We shiver in the bare, temporary room where she has
come
for transfusion. I drowse over my coffee.
It's not like that, she declares.
I rouse; arch an eyebrow in response.
Angels. She gestures toward the TV as
her IV tubes arc out and glitter. *Not at all.*

She ought to know. My mother once died
and went to Heaven. In a coma for three weeks,
one long night set off bells and alarms for the ICU.
She told anyone who would listen that she ascended
through pink clouds that smelled of roses to meet Jesus,
who she assured us would nowadays be detained
at any airport, looked nothing like in Sunday School.
She asked if she had gained Heaven.
Jesus assured her it would be whatever she desired
paradise to be, but not yet. He sent her home,
"you're not done suffering yet."

Angels brought me back. Big scary angels with nary
a feather in sight. People have it wrong
when they show pretty women and fat baby angels.
Was anybody in the Bible glad to see angels? Mostly not,
Jacob wrestled his, Sarah laughed at hers, Lot's scared
him enough to flee Sodom dragging his family. Mary met
Gabriel, that poor little girl. Just imagine. The shepherds
in Bethlehem were sore afraid. Them angels in the lion's den

and fiery furnace weren't fellows to mess with, no,
or the one set at the gates of Eden with a fiery sword.

She falls back into meds and sleeps. I study
angels on my phone, find that only
cherubim and seraphim sprout wings.
I ponder archangels, find Gabriel and Michael,
learn Raphael and Uriel of the flaming sword.
The Kabbalah names seven: one with the glorious
name, Metatron, fit for a superhero.

We, created less than the angels, reduced them,
rendered them as harp-wielding and infantile.
Should I, like the psalmist, call on angels for help,
I want a being who can stand in the presence of God,
who bears a sword, or commands a voice like a lion,
to be the agent of Providence and the harbinger of grace.

JANE HICKS

CHANGELING

When sorrow comes to your bed
like a just-weaned child, remember
sharp teeth and an appetite too large
to succor. It has its own bed, its own
place, so you both rest, so in the light
of day you give it what it needs,
not what it wants.

It may have the face of love
but sorrow thinks only
of itself, wails in the dark
where it must learn to sleep.

JANE HICKS

SAFETY OF SMALL THINGS

Deadfall disallows glimpses and visits
with deer and woodpeckers.
The squirrels and chipmunks, near frantic,
ignore the hiker on the path.
The fox has gone to ground.
A rain moves through.
The pin oaks rattle and branches clack;
the wind worries the ridge. On the lee side,
an inch worm measures a shelf fungus.

Here, a night nest, warm wallow
in the tall grass that edges the brush pile—
a deliberate thicket composed for the safety
of small things. Tunnels and trails,
marked by tufts of hair and feathers,
lead to an unseen world that flourishes
while I sleep.

JANE HICKS

BOREAS

The broom sedge hissing by the fence,
the cows walking heads down
toward the south pasture,
a starling mending the raveling hem
of a shawl lifting, warping
above the hills—

I felt the cold burn,
but Daddy was freezing
from the inside out.

Warily I stepped around his bluster:
I couldn't do a damned thing right.
Praying for his angry soul,
I didn't understand that every word
was like a match smoking in the wind,
the old god roaring over the Blue Ridge.

JOHN THOMAS YORK

AN *APPALACHIAN HERITAGE* INTERVIEW WITH

SONJA LIVINGSTON

In essayist Sonja Livingston's latest collection *Ladies Night at the Dreamland* (University of Georgia Press), the Appalachian native of western New York explores the lives of historical women—famous, notorious, and invented—and in many ways her own life and understanding of herself. Through re-imaginings of figures like Virginia Dare ("Dare"), Luna Fugate ("Blue Kentucky Girl"), and Alice Mitchell and Freda Ward, two young women in Memphis who fell in love and attempted to elope ("Mad Love: The Ballad of Fred and Allie"), Livingston confronts and explores the often difficult to navigate invisible spaces between existences—love and cultural acceptance, race, immigration, and the tension of home and away, and geography.

Appalachian Heritage interviewed Sonja Livingston during a two-week email exchange about her body of work, her latest collection and the themes of raising the veil of hidden experiences and geographical identity. Louisville-based writer and editor Beth Newberry conducted the interview with Livingston who was in Cork, Ireland, teaching a month-long nonfiction workshop with the University of New Orleans. The interview has been edited for length.

■■■

BETH NEWBERRY: You are in Ireland this summer—what took you there? Do any of the landscapes you've seen there remind you of the places you call home?

SONJA LIVINGSTON: I've been in Cork and the surrounding towns in western Ireland, seeing lots of green pastures and jagged coastline and sea. The interior landscape reminds me of Kentucky, all the green hills broken by old barns and grazing cattle. But while I feel very much at home in Kentucky, it isn't my home. In fact, Ireland doesn't remind me necessarily of any home I've ever had, but does it feel familiar. People talk about connecting to certain landscapes and ancestral memory and all that, but I tend to be cynical. But then I descended in Ireland for the first time and found myself surrounded by the patchwork of fields and [I] choked up right there on the plane. Something about the place is special. Not only the fields and cliffs, but the cadence of the language, the music, the history—even the poverty and struggle. I've been fortunate to travel many places, but Ireland is where I want to return to again and again.

BN: I'd like to talk a bit about your piece "Blue Kentucky Girl" which is in your new book *Ladies Night at the Dreamland,* but was also published in *Appalachian Heritage* [Summer 2014 issue]. It's a captivating piece that is lyrical, personal and interactive with history. I actually read it for the first time when I was on Troublesome Creek—a place mentioned in the essay—in Hindman, Kentucky, at the Appalachian Writers' Workshop. Your storytelling about Luna [one the "Blue Fugates"], her life and family was very intuitive, detailed and avoided stereotypes and judgments often associated with this story of the region. Have you spent time in eastern Kentucky or in tight-knit rural or Appalachian communities?

SL: Thank you! In terms of avoiding stereotypes, I think the job of the writer—especially the nonfiction writer—is to get to the place beyond easy categories and judgments. The desire to show people and places that are often hidden or misunderstood drives a great deal of my writing. As someone who grew up in a family and setting that are very easily judged (often harshly and incorrectly) I'm especially sensitive to those things, the wrong they do, and the ways they falsely divide us.

I spent my childhood in rural portions of western New York, in parts of the state which some have called Appalachia. I've described it as the place where northern tip of Appalachia meets up with the easternmost notch of the Rust Belt. I'm not sure how or where the region fits exactly, except to say

Sonja Livingston

that the culture of rural West Virginia and eastern Kentucky do feel familiar. My mother grew up in the mountains of New Hampshire. We tend to think of New England as posh and clam-shelled, but the way she grew up in the mountains and the stories she tells also remind me [of] Appalachian stories, the hard work and limited resources. I drew on her experiences and my own childhood in rural environments, as well as visits to Appalachian communities.

I don't mean to suggest that these places are interchangeable. They are each rich in their own traditions and history, and yet, living as a child without indoor plumbing in Batavia, New York, let me understand something about my mother's experiences in the White Mountains and yes, even something of what it would have been like for Luna in eastern Kentucky.

In terms of her unusual color, well, I knew about being different and again. I drew on my experiences as a white child who lived for a time on Seneca reservation and later in a largely non-white inner-city neighborhood to think about skin color and difference. In the end, I used a combination of research, experience and imagination as a way to try to know more about the people and places I write about, including Luna and Troublesome Creek.

BN: I'm also curious as to how this piece evolved. There are some very strong connections drawn between the narrator's experience and Luna's—a conversation between the two characters almost. Did you write the sections about your own life in conjunction or response to research about the Fugates? Or did the threads of the story develop separately at first?

SL: I wrote about Luna first. Her story really captivated me. I wanted to know more about her and how she'd lived, but I also wanted to explore why and how she'd captured my attention so thoroughly. What I've come to discover in writing about various women's lives is that the while objective is to know the other person better, in doing so, we inevitably come to know something more of ourselves. In other words, I wasn't interested in writing straight biography. I wanted to combine what was already known with what I most wanted to know in a sort of conversation with each woman, and in this case, Luna.

Over time, the essay developed but didn't seem done. I'd written about Luna but still couldn't place why she mattered so much to me and especially why now. So much of writing is letting things percolate in your head, so eventually, I let go of trying so hard and the connection naturally arose. Skin color matters in our culture. No matter how much we talk or don't talk about it, it remains a part of who we are as Americans, and in my own life, labels and divisions according to race and class have been central.

BN: I [want] to follow up your comment about the geography of your childhood and this understanding you've cultivated about "places that are often hidden or misunderstood," which I see as a direct correlation to how you describe western New York: "as the place where northern tip of Appalachia meets up with the easternmost notch of the Rust Belt. I'm not sure how or where the region fits exactly."

I think that in terms of geography (and also other things that stratify people like class and culture) the expectation

is that people are one thing or another—you are urban or rural, you are industrial or agriculture, you are a hick or you are sophisticated. And when a place such as western New York, or a person with multiple and varied geographies, can't be just one thing or the other, certain identities can get lost or hidden when interacting with the dominant culture or individuals. Do you now feel, or have you previously felt, caught between places or cultures and how have you navigated that as a writer?

SL: What a great question. In some ways, the idea of being caught between categories (of class, regional identity, race) seems like an obvious consequence of our diverse culture. That said, I don't think we make allowances for how many of us are caught in those in-between spaces. But to answer your question, I do feel caught between categories, most especially in terms of class. When *Ghostbread* [Livingston's first book, which won the Association of Writers and Writing Program Prize for Nonfiction] was published and people began to invite me to read at their colleges and organizations, the question I could always count on was: "How did you get out of poverty?" I struggled (and still struggle) to answer because there's no solid line to step over and be done with something like poverty. Many people in my family are still poor. Most of the people I grew up with are still struggling. I still battle an almost automatic sense of shame and not belonging.

I just watched an interview with the writer Frank McCourt who said that giving people money and food doesn't touch the real poverty, which is deeply ingrained—the sort of hunger that takes more than a full cupboard to heal. Class is not black or white, yet the ways we've learned to speak of it is exactly as if its various categories can be inhabited neatly and fully.

I've lived and taught in Memphis for the past six years and will begin teaching [at] Virginia Commonwealth University in Richmond this fall. As a writer, I was drawn to a graduate writing program with a southern school because the South and its writers have a pull on me. But I'm from the North. What does this mean? To be from the North? It means plenty, of course, but it also doesn't mean as much as one might think. I'm interested in this terrain. The territory that refuses to fit neatly into categories can be tough to live with, especially when we're children who want so desperately to fit in, but it's gold for writers.

What can't people tell by looking at you? I often ask this question to students as a writing prompt—because, of course, what think we see in others is not always what lies beneath the surface. The space between what others perceive about us and what is true is most fertile ground. It provides an opportunity to know ourselves and each other in ways that shake up those superficial categories and actually mean something.

BN: Your work both in *Ghostbread* and *Ladies Night at the Dreamland* has a lot of intersections of what is seen and what is hidden, whether its the supernatural or forbidden love or even the parallel lives that exist when people are separated by distance or death, like when you write in "Twyla": "But what is ever really gone forever?"). I was wondering if you could talk about the interplay of the seen and unseen in one of [the] pieces in your latest collection?

SL: Several of the essays bring up that idea: What is ever really gone forever? Perhaps these essays were a way for me to show that where there's attention, nothing is gone forever. But that's only half-true. Some things are tougher to reclaim—there's

Livingston's latest book was published in March.

no way of knowing the inner lives of others, for instance, especially those who lived so quietly and are long-gone. The best we can do is to use what's known to make a guess. In terms of the interplay between what is seen and unseen, as I said earlier, it's a rich ground for writing. In writing about the lives of women, especially, what is seen and known versus what's hidden is not only rich, but very telling.

For instance, "The Opposite of Fear" weaves together the story of the young woman who crossed Niagara Falls on a tightrope in 1876, with rumination on my own tendency to be timid. The segments that focus on Maria Spelterini show her up on that rope, flaming in her vibrant costume and straddling the space between land and sky. And while it was Maria's daredevil act that captured my attention, I really wanted to know who she was off that tightrope. That's the part that was hidden, even for someone who stood so fully in the spotlight. She crossed the tightrope a few times, then promptly disappeared, so that even those few women who lived outside the expectations of time and place and left a record of their acts, are very little known. Was Maria really brave, or so desperate she had no choice but to get up on that tightrope and walk over the Niagara River Gorge at a time when women couldn't even legally cast a vote?

The essays in *Ladies Night at the Dreamland* vary widely in terms of subject, scope, and form, but what binds them together is this divide between being seen and being known, and what that might say about these women's lives (and by extension, perhaps, our own).

BN: I first read "A Thousand Mary Doyles" in your book, but a friend in my writer's group read it first in [the online

literary journal] *Brevity* and talks still about how much life and story you fit into 527 words—yes, she cites a word count from memory. It is quite an evocative and expansive piece for its length. It reminded me (as did *Ghostbread*) of one of my first loves of literature as a young writer, Sandra Cisneros's novel *The House on Mango Street.* Both paint colorful pictures with a small amount of text that reveals character, place and desire. Do you see "A Thousand Mary Doyles" as a piece of flash nonfiction? From a craft perspective, how are you able to traverse so much story and geography it such few words?

SL: Well, thank you and thank you to your friend! "A Thousand Mary Doyles" is flash non-fiction. I tend to write short pieces, and always have, even before I understood what to call them. Once I began taking writing classes and reading more literary nonfiction, I recognized that these pieces were brief essays.

Short pieces provide a natural fit for my process and my content. Memory tends to arrive in powerful images or fragments versus complete narratives. Part of what I love about writing from memory is trying to understand certain images and experiences stay with us. When I was writing *Ghostbread,* for instance, I'd remember something—such as the hand-me-down Kung Fu lunch box that I hated—and wrote specifically about that memory as fully as I could before moving onto the next.

Whether they stand on their own or are strung together in a book or a longer essays, flash essays often function like snapshots that allow writers to zoom in on one image or moment and mine it for all its worth. These 'snapshots' can stand on their own but they can also serve as a stand in for many moments. When I describe a hand-me-down Kung-Fu lunch box, in *Ghostbread,* for instance, I don't need to describe the hand-me-down sweater or the hand-me-down running shoes. The reader understands that the lunch box implies many other things.

It's probably no coincidence that I enjoy photography. We human beings have an excess of information coming at us—we see and hear and touch so much in a day. A short essay provides a way to manage and frame and convey what we notice. I try to use every tool available to me (language, sentence length, verb tense, sensory details, etc.) in the same way a photographer makes use of angle, shadow, and light. ■

BROTHERS 6 & 8

Already I wear the many heads
    of a trickster god

loose-fitted like a cheap mask
    on fright night.

Monkey me is playful
    when you are sad.

Poke your neck, knuckle your head,
    tickle your bottom rib

until you choke. When I'm wolf faced
    green and yellow eyed

my teeth get sharp on the bone rope
    of your spine.

I swear the bull's broad shoulders are base
    enough for you to jump.

Brother trust your body to this web:
    come to my praying hands.

I want what you want, someone
    to hold so close

we forget ourselves as one—we become
    many, we become more.

CHRISTOPHER MCCURRY

BROTHERS 12 & 14

Chained in her pen
our dog died in the flood.

You cry because you love her
and she loved you back.

I don't cry because I hate
the stake, the chain, the dog.

Each one a tether.

Hundreds of water blackened
leaves hang on the fence.

Their stripped veins
worshipful hands

reaching for the world
jerked away. We hear

on the news that rescue
crews couldn't find

the mother or the child
swept to where we all

eventually follow.

Some bent low
like grass,

others strung out
like a dead dog.

CHRISTOPHER MCCURRY

BROTHERS 22 & 24

You used to have all these
impossible to answer questions

like why angels, why one
who falls and one

who rises from the grave
now you think you know

when I told you my daughter
would be born in seven months

I didn't say we spent a day
thinking about killing her

you know the rest
she was born

she died anyway
I've got some questions

that are impossible to answer
like who cares about Job

and his shit life
does my capacity for suffering

explain its necessity
each death is its own

ocean of grief unto itself
she had one breath

in the photo we took
she was dead already

Give me a heavy stone, brother
I've a body in need of rebirth

CHRISTOPHER MCCURRY

MUDDIN'

LAURA LEIGH MORRIS

Though they weren't married anymore, Chelle and Bill still got together for sex from time to time. But only when they had both been drinking at the Elks, usually on nights when the special was tequila. Cheap tequila with a little lime and salt was Chelle's favorite. After the first few shots, when Chelle said, "That's it for me—I don't want to crawl home,"

Bill would send a shot over to her table, then another. He would bring the third one himself.

They still liked each other when they were sober, but they only remembered how much they'd been in love when they were drunk. Then, it was as if they were still in high school and a bottle of Matador and a starry sky were all they needed to believe they were meant to be together. The wedding they'd had after a positive pregnancy test, the stillbirth months later, the intervening years of loving and hating each other until the hate outweighed the love—all that disappeared when Bill bought her drinks and put his hand on her leg under the table. Then, they remembered the nights Chelle had stopped believing she killed their baby and the years they'd spent trying to make a new one. Eventually, Chelle had come to believe she was defective. That was when the love had turned into hate. It had been a relief to end the marriage when they were thirty; there was no point in trying to make something work that obviously didn't. But every once in a while, when the sky was clear and the tequila went down smoothly, they were eighteen again, and what mattered most was getting each other's clothes off as quickly as possible.

"Let's go muddin," Chelle said one night after sex. They were at her house, formerly their house, in her bed, which had also been their marriage bed. Bill lay on his back, still breathing heavily, but that was more from years of smoking and working in the coal mines than from the sex, which had been quick and unimaginative. He sat up, lit two cigarettes, and passed one to her.

"I'm too drunk," Bill said.

"You're just the right amount of drunk." Chelle swung her leg around and sat on Bill's chest, straddling him. "It'll be like it used to be."

At the moment, she was almost drunk enough to believe it and that their fifteen minutes of sex had been like it was years before. Then they'd made love for hours, or at least touched and licked each other for hours, kept each other excited for whole nights.

"Your car?" Bill asked.

"Still at the Elks."

"Okay," he said. "But I'm driving."

"We always were good together," she said.

"We still are."

Chelle didn't bother with a bra—she threw a sweatshirt over jeans and called it enough. It was still early spring, and though the days were warm enough for a T-shirt, the nights still dipped into the forties. Tonight, the moon was new and the sky was clear, millions of stars twinkling above them. With no cloud cover, it was also cold enough to see your breath, and

But every once in a while, when the sky was clear and the tequila went down smoothly, they were eighteen again...

the weatherman had called for frost. As soon as Bill turned the key in the ignition, Chelle switched the heat to full blast.

Bill turned on the headlights and aimed them toward the trees. Chelle's double-wide sat on an acre of land surrounded by forest. She didn't own anything outside of that one cleared acre, but the Millers up the road let her use the woods when she wanted, except during deer season. Then, she wore orange even in her yard.

"Hold on tight," Bill yelled as they sped into the trees.

The truck jumped forward, plunging into mud holes and climbing out the other side, mud flying into the air, onto the windshield and back onto the truck. Bill turned on the wipers, but they just spread the mess, making it even harder to see. But that was part of the fun, moving between trees, sinking into the mud and then spinning the tires until you popped out, flying across the forest floor until you got hung up again and had to work your way out, never knowing exactly what was in front of you.

Ahead, Chelle saw what looked like a small pond. "Don't," she said.

"Don't what?"

"It's too deep. We'll get stuck."

Bill laughed, a booming belly laugh that filled the cab of the truck. Then, he gunned it, and Chelle's stomach lifted and dropped as the truck plunged into the mud, curtains of water spraying up, enveloping the windows. They climbed out of the hole, tires spinning, motor whining, and continued farther into the woods.

They were approaching areas Chelle had never seen before, beyond the Millers' land, onto someone else's, miles from Chelle's house. They sped up, the forest flashing by more quickly, saplings smacking the bumper and then disappearing. The truck bucked over mounds of earth, tree roots, and anything else that got in its way. Bill let out a yell as the truck slid across muddy grass and sideswiped a tree, knocking the side mirror off. Soon, Chelle was yelling along with him, both whooping at the darkness, feeling like the only ones alive in the empty night.

"I love you, baby," Bill yelled, and she said, "I love you, too." In that moment, they meant it.

There was another small pond ahead, but Chelle didn't yell out, and the truck dove into it easily enough, curtains of muddy water covering them again. But this time, when Bill gunned the engine to climb out the other side, the tires didn't catch hold. They spun in the mud, spewing water and chunks of earth behind them, while the truck sank into the muck. Bill downshifted and tried again, but the truck only settled more deeply into the earth.

"Wait," Chelle yelled over the whine of the motor, and Bill stopped and swore. Now almost completely underwater, the headlights dimmed. Chelle looked down and saw that the water had risen into the cab, covering her feet. She climbed onto the seat, but it was too late—her canvas sneakers were completely drenched. "Goddammit, Bill," she said, but he ignored her.

"I can't open the door," he said. He stuck his head out the window.

"No shit. I'll go out the back." Chelle opened the window in the back of the cab, and Bill pushed her through. It was cold enough that she could see her breath. The stars were bright above her. She shivered and wrapped her arms around her chest, cursing herself for not bringing a jacket.

Already, muddy water had started to seep through the tailgate and into the bed. She peered over the side and saw that the tires were almost completely buried in mud.

She rushed back to the window. "Turn it off, Bill."

"It's cold," he said. He held his hands over the heating vents. "Get back in so I can close the window."

She stuck one leg and then another through the window and said, "You've gotta turn the truck off."

"It's too damn cold for that."

"The water's too high. The exhaust is covered. You're gonna kill us."

He turned and looked out the back, peering past the bed. "You sure?"

In answer, she turned the key, and the truck was silent.

"I was gonna do it," Bill said.

"Not fast enough."

"It wouldn't kill us that quick."

Chelle's buzz had been wearing off for a while, and now she had a headache. "How do you know?" she asked.

"I just do. Besides, do you smell anything?"

"Carbon monoxide doesn't smell."

"Exhaust does."

Chelle leaned back and closed her eyes. "Did you bring your phone? We're gonna need a tow."

"No," Bill said. "We'll have to walk out."

"What about pushing it?"

"And how am I supposed to do that?"

"The usual way—you push, and I'll steer. Maybe the wheels can catch onto something."

"You saw how deep we are, didn't you?" he asked.

"We can still try," she said. It was cold and late, and she wanted to be back in her bed. Alone. She was too old for this.

"You push then. I'm not getting covered in mud."

"No way," she said.

"Exactly." He leaned back and crossed his arms over his chest. "We'll have to walk."

"Now?" Chelle asked.

"In the morning," Bill said.

"What am I supposed to do 'til then?"

"Keep warm."

Chelle was shivering in her thin sweatshirt and wet shoes. "That's easy for you to say. You've got extra insulation." She looked at Bill and the weight he'd put on since their divorce—his gut was bigger, and he had a layer of fat around his face and neck.

"Well, look at you sitting there like you're something special," he said. He smirked at her, one eyebrow raised, arms crossed. "Not all of us think eating's bad. You lose any more weight and you're gonna look like an orange skeleton, all that tanning. Ever think of eating a burger?"

"I eat," she yelled. "I can't help it." She'd always been skinny, no matter what she ate. And not sexy skinny either. She hadn't gotten boobs or her period until she was sixteen, and her hips had never filled out. She was built like a kid and still had to buy pants in the girls' section at the store. It was embarrassing walking around with glitter and stars on the butt of your jeans, but those were the only ones that fit.

Bill looked her up and down. "Well, it ain't working. There's no cushion for the pushin."

"Fuck you too," she said. "Mr. God-of-all-men. With that belly and the hair on your shoulders, I'm sure you have women everywhere trying to get on you."

"At least I don't go around pretending I'm perfect," he said. "You act like your shit don't stink, and now you're looking at me like it's all my fault we're out here. Remember, you're the one who wanted to go muddin."

"I've never pretended I don't make mistakes," Chelle said. "I didn't say it was all your fault. I'll take my share of the blame."

"Like when you told me you only married me because you were knocked up?"

She lost her breath. "I didn't mean that," she said finally. "Not really."

He didn't answer or look in her direction.

"We both said a lot of things we didn't mean," she said.

"I'm going to try to get some sleep," he said. He leaned back in the seat, wrapped his arms around himself, and closed his eyes.

Chelle curled into a ball, but she couldn't get warm. She kicked her shoes off and stuck her bare feet in a crack in the seat. Then she pulled her arms inside her sweatshirt and wrapped them around her body to conserve heat. She pulled her shirt over her mouth, breathing warm air onto her chest, but the moisture made her shiver. Her whole body shook, and she couldn't stop.

"We were good together for a little while, weren't we?" Bill asked.

"For a few years, I'd say." She looked at him, but his eyes were still closed.

"You ever think what would've happened if we hadn't lost the baby?"

"I try not to," she said. Bill looked at her then, but Chelle turned away. "I did that enough when we were married."

"Do you—"

"Let's just try to get some sleep, okay?" she asked.

"Okay," Bill said. He looked at her, and she met his gaze. "Okay."

"I'm just tired," she said and leaned her head against the side window.

Though the truck had a bench seat, she tried to keep herself as far from Bill as possible. Sometimes, it hurt being this close to him. When they were drunk, they were fine, good together even, but when they were sober, as she was now, a lot of hurt came through. A lot of love as well, but she couldn't always separate the two. Tonight they felt like the same thing.

Chelle looked out the window, but between the trees and lack of moonlight, she couldn't even guess the way back to civilization. The stars glowed enough to see a few feet in front of her but not enough to judge which direction to take. Out here, houses sat on fifty or a hundred acres and you could walk for hours without running into another person if you didn't know where you were going.

"You won't make it back on your own," Bill said, as though reading her mind.

"I might."

"No," he said. "You won't. As soon as it's light, we'll be on our way."

"Watch me," Chelle said and tried to push the door open, but the water and mud had sealed it shut.

"Baby," Bill said. "Baby, please."

He reached for her, but Chelle shrunk against the door. "I'm not your baby," she said. "Let's just go to sleep." She pulled her knees to her chest again but couldn't stop shivering.

"You want to curl up together? We'll both stay warmer," Bill said.

She looked over, and Bill was watching her. She shook her head and turned away.

"It's gonna be a long night," he said.

It was cold enough that even the forest's normal nighttime noises were missing. Everything had dug a hole, built a nest,

Chelle looked out the window, but between the trees and lack of moonlight, she couldn't even guess the way back to civilization.

bundled up, and hunkered down for the night. Chelle and Bill were alone. She propped her back against the door, facing him.

"Have you dated anyone since we split up?" she asked.

"Dated?"

"Or slept with," she said.

"I slept with a couple women," he said.

"Oh."

"Did you think I wouldn't?"

"I never thought about it 'til now," she said.

"They weren't dates. They were both just one night." He was quiet. Then, "How about you?"

"I dated one guy for a while," she said.

"And?" Bill asked.

"He liked to travel, and he talked about the trips we'd take. I realized he could give me the kind of life I always dreamed of, the one we could never afford."

"I couldn't help getting laid off those times," Bill said.

"I'm not blaming you," Chelle said. "The thing is, this man offered me everything I thought I wanted."

"He sounds perfect," Bill said. There was an edge to his voice.

Chelle nodded. "Almost," she said. "But his hands were too soft. Like he'd never done a day of real work in his life. I wanted to hand him a shovel or something."

"I ruined you," Bill said.

"Yeah," Chelle said. "I guess you did."

She leaned her head back and closed her eyes. Bill pulled her feet out of the crack in the seat and rubbed them between his calloused hands. Chelle let him. She sat on her side of the truck's cab, he on his, but her feet had crossed into his territory, and Bill kept them warm. Like that, with one touch over years of distance, they fell asleep. ■

KATYDID

Green leaf's staccato
in summer's heat
unseen but heard

like a hiss keeping its
bliss as an ostinato of urge.
This instinct itches air

alive in whisper and distinct
as dream till it sings a shrill
chant distilling the dark.

Its two-note syllable
an angel's green declension,
a season's mean inflection

that begins in spring's silence
as a grey scab hidden on the underside
of stem till it rises as

the harbinger of heat
on beech and maple, oak
and long-needled pine,

a savory nymph that by July
will keep the night seared white
in song until September's dying light

leaves its green beneath the forest's
floor to survive until first frost's
sacrifice in starlight

its final rite of becoming
the way all gods must die
in their understory of urge

until they're released
from the green world
into this trinity of one.

CHAPMAN HOOD FRAZIER

GIFTS OF THE SOUTH

An Eclipse

The moon, red
like fat dripping
from the porterhouse
side of the T-Bone,
an American God
in its own rites.
Beef moon, nurturing
our ebb and flow
with hands that knead
us to tenderness
and umami. Then,
a cleanse, clean as gin
straight up tasting like
clear night sky.

A Supercell

I thought it too much
to cull storms, but flailed
hail that punctured metal
rooftops. I spun wind
with my wanting
into the fabric of air.
In that brief hour
of power outage, a moment
to rest under blue stars.

A Meteor Shower

Dust flung by the Big
Dipper, Ursa Major,
radiance at Camelopardalis.
The storm gifted two
meteors the size of fireflies—
fat, slow and glowing
over Tennessee, while
the rest of the humble
scatter lit black grass
in rolling foothills of Appalachia.

A Pastime

Moonshine—a mash
of corn and taste of dirt.
My home in glass diorama,
soon to be an empty vessel.
I tilt back my head
impossibly far until southern
roots set fire to my
throat and make still
the sounds of chords.

CHRISTOPHER PETRUCELLI

BIRMINGHAM

Vulcan rises from the black top.
Both hands forming the other,
fingers work loose pig iron into arms.

The Buick, rusted and scraped, rattles
down I-65 where the rolling hills
level out like a gasping bellow.

The hands squeeze, work
white-hot metal and mold legs
to torso with scratches and scores.

On 5th Avenue I had my first taste of
deep south, the air so wet it became
waterfire—throat and skin scorched.

Hammer to the ground, spear to sky,
knees bleeding with slag, Vulcan
stands above Red Mountain.

That night I saw Charon in the hot mist
paddling over the bar, his boat made more clear
with each drag of a cigarette, each blow of smoke.

CHRISTOPHER PETRUCELLI

THE GREAT FLOOD

Hazard, Kentucky is no different
than a hundred rural towns
started as a trading post,
funded by coal that turned lungs

and hands dark at the start
of the twentieth century.
And while I love the story
of Hazard folk making

the Stone Gap journey,
having to go over
Big Black Mountain, it isn't
the shantytowns left behind

when businesses went bust,
or the lung cancer cases,
either, that draw me.
It's the dust and the mud

I come to see. The same
dust and mud that always
claim this town, where history
is marked by the water

that's made Hazard its own—
the Great Flood of '27,
the Great Flood of '37,
and the black magic sevens go on

into the Great Flood of '57
and...where before meteorologists,
people could predict
the size of the maelstrom coming

by watching the dust swirl
in the middle of the streets,
a dirty gypsy-like
fortune-telling dance,

with small bits of gravel
and earth twisting around
before, overhead, the clouds'
bulk fell in grey blocks

to the ground until the nearby
Kentucky River bred
and claimed a new space,
making a Venetian world

where no public roads survived,
just miles and miles of mud. Archived
photographs have captured this
murky, wet distress: "Note the automobile

barely visible under the flood waters,"
says the back of one. "Looking across
the river from town, see the iron bridge,"
says another, "to the train depot that lays destroyed,"

and my personal favorite, "A view up Main Street
where Rita's and Jonnie's Diner is destroyed"
written on the last. I don't know why I like it
so much, except that I can imagine

Rita and Jonnie, not unlike my own family
from these Eastern Kentucky parts, their determined
pupils paying homage when dilated
to round pieces of coal.

I see them methodically boarding up
their restaurant, still holding
sand bags in their hands as the water
starts to ooze through the door.

LANA AUSTIN

THE PIG

Now, you'd think
if he had enough sense
to get up there,
he'd have enough sense
to get back down.
The archived photograph
deifies him enough to give him
the benefit of the doubt,
standing up there in 1957
on that filing cabinet God-like.
Reminds me of the Stonewall statue,
the pig astride a filing cabinet
and Jackson on his horse, both
of them with muscles tight
and if they were dogs,
their hackles would be up.
He must've used the office chair
that was found floating
around the room
to get to his metal refuge.
And that must've been why
he couldn't get down.
Those witch-possessed
Hazard, Kentucky waters
rose so much that even something
fairly big like an office chair
could just float away.
Huge things could drift
around, too, like cars. We're not

talking about today's tiny
Ford Fiestas. We mean behemoth
gas-guzzlers with testosterone-infused
names like Thunderbird,
emasculated, bobbing
around in the flood
as if they were a little boy's toy
boats in the bathtub.
Whatever you do,
don't call the pig cute.

LANA AUSTIN

ROBBING THE HEADLINES
REPURPOSING TRUE EVENTS IN FICTION

AMANDA JO RUNYON

Early in the semester, my Appalachian literature students had the opportunity to have a Skype conversation with author Silas House. They had just finished reading his novel *A Parchment of Leaves,* and I hoped they would ask him meaningful and intelligent questions about the novel, questions that would lead to a deeper understanding of themes and characters or good writing in general. Unsurprisingly, one of the first questions that came from the group was, *where do you get your ideas?* Many writers and instructors squirm at this question. It doesn't necessarily indicate to the author that you have read and thought about their material, nor does it engage the particular craft decisions writers spend painstaking hours making. It could be considered a generic, blanket question. In the essay, "Where Do You Get Your Ideas?" Alice Mattison says readers ask this question of writers as if authors might respond, "I order them online" or "In the supermarket, near the pancake mix."[1] Admittedly, it is a common question, but it is also an important and valid question, particularly for the writer of fiction. Mattison agrees that the curiosity of readers is understandable. She says, "everything about writing is suspect; we may as well face that. Making up a story out of nothing is something like trafficking in the occult."[2] But no fiction story is ever made up "out of nothing." Ideas for fiction come from life, from the experiences or observations of the author in the real world. The real question, then, is how do fiction writers decide how much of the real world to use in their invented stories?

When I was a graduate student at Morehead State University, the instructor for my Advanced Fiction Workshop, Crystal Wilkinson, asked our class to think about what haunts us as writers. What images or themes do we find reoccurring on our pages? These things, she suggested, could be where we draw our ideas. Later, in a fiction workshop at the Mountain Heritage Literary Festival, I heard Gwyn Hyman Rubio lecture on how to forage for ideas. Rubio suggested good writers are often thieves. We could rob from the cradle; that is, we could write stories about our own pasts, particularly, our childhoods. Rubio's second suggestion was that writers could rob the grave for ideas, or write the stories of their ancestors. Finally, she said, we could rob other authors, relying on a variation of a theme we've encountered in other books.

In my own fiction, I have robbed ideas from the cradle, the grave, and the themes of other authors, but during Rubio's lecture I found myself thinking back to Crystal Wilkinson's workshop question, and realized that none of these things haunt my writing. I am haunted by the stories of true events that occur in the community around me. I spend a lot of time in the archives of my university, scouring old newspapers and photographs that give me insight to events that have shaped

To repurpose a true event into a fictional story, an author must figure out how to change the event into something new.

and influenced my hometown. I am fascinated by events that have such dramatic effect on a community that they are remembered and passed down, in some variation, for years. I have a tendency to, as Rubio might phrase it, rob the headlines.

To understand how I might use true stories in my own work, I need to shift the focus from where I get ideas to how I use ideas. I write about actual events, not to recreate them, but to repurpose them. According to the Merriam-Webster Dictionary, to repurpose is to "change something so it can be used for a different purpose." An image search of the verb will result in pictures of crib beds transformed into hallway benches, kitchen forks turned into windchimes, or other common, household items made into something new. Recently, a friend gave me a gift of a wreath made out of an old copy of *The Dollmaker* by Harriette Arnow. The idea is that once an object has lived out its use in one form, it can be remade, not into the same object, but into something new, to be used in new ways.

To repurpose a true event into a fictional story, an author must figure out how to change the event into something new. The difference, then, does not necessarily lie in the details, but in the function of the story. Since we all derive ideas from some aspect of life, we can imagine all writing on a spectrum that ranges from factual nonfiction to wholly invented fiction. Writers who repurpose events must decide where their stories will fall on this spectrum and what approaches to use to blend facts with imagination.

In *Quiet Dell*, Jayne Anne Phillips tells the story of highly publicized murders and the subsequent trial that occurred in West Virginia in 1931. Asta Eicher was a widowed mother of three living in Illinois when she placed an advertisement for companionship in the Lonely Hearts section of the newspaper. Through the advertisement, she met Cornelius Pierson, a man who presented himself as wealthy and charismatic in his letters. Pierson, known elsewhere as Harry Powers, would gain the trust of Asta and eventually murder her along with her three children, Annabel, Hart, and Grethe. The bodies of the Eicher family were found buried beneath a garage that Powers owned in Quiet Dell, West Virginia, along with the body of another woman who corresponded with Powers via letters.

Phillips's novel uses an interesting blend of fact and imagination to create a full dramatization of the story. In the acknowledgements at the end of the novel, Phillips states that only four characters from the book are "wholly invented": Asta's mother-in-law, Lavinia, reporters Emily Thornhill and Eric Lindstrom, and the young boy who eventually becomes Emily's adopted son, Randolph Mason Phillips.[3] The other characters in the novel, which outside of the Eicher family, includes a close family friend and boarder, a concerned banker, and a crew of West Virginia lawmen, are historical. In an essay on her website called "Concerning Quiet Dell," Phillips says, "The names of the characters whose lives the crime claimed or influenced are real: their thoughts, perceptions, and relationships are imagined."[4] Phillips maintains the basic facts of who her characters were and what happened to them, but she goes a step further by creating an internal world for all the characters that she could not have possibly researched.

Phillips begins her dramatization with the first person point of view of nine-year-old Annabel, to whom the novel is dedicated. In the first chapter, Annabel introduces the members of her family and lays the framework for the family's story. She begins, "When the year turns, there are bells on the wind. All the old years fall on the ground in lights. When you walk across those lights, it sounds like walking on all the piled-up leaves of giant trees. But up high the bells are ringing for everyone alive." Annabel's grandmother has told her about the bells, which her mother claims is "just a story," but Annabel asserts, "I always do hear the bells."[5] We see immediately that Annabel is an imaginative, whimsical child, and that her grandmother, Lavinia, encourages her fanciful ideas, while her mother is uncertain how to handle her daughter's precocious imagination. By introducing the novel with Annabel's imagined story of the bells, Phillips prepares us for the mix and invention that is to come.

In the first half of the novel, the point of view changes with every short chapter. We get a section of close third person point of view of the family friend and long-time boarder,

1 Alice Mattison. "Where Do You Get Your Ideas?" *The Writer's Chronicle*, February 2012, accessed 17 February 2016, https://www.awpwriter.org/magazine_media/writers_chronicle_view/1515/where_do_you_get_your_ideas

2 Ibid.

3 Jayne Anne Phillips. *Quiet Dell: A Novel* (London: Vintage, 2014), 439.

4 Jayne Anne Phillips. "Concerning *Quiet Dell*," accessed 20 March 2016, http://jayneannephillips.com/quiet-dell/authors-note/

5 Phillips, *Quiet Dell*, 3.

Charles O'Doyle. Charles's section begins with his reflection on the relationship he shares with Asta Eicher. He calls her the "sister he'd wished for," so close that they had no secrets and O'Doyle was given permission to call her by her pet name, Anna.[6] We learn that Lavinia has passed away, and that Asta is struggling financially. Though Charles is secretly homosexual, he plans to propose marriage to Asta in order to save her from her financial troubles and add stability to his own life. He wants "to protect this family, cosset them," and claims, "theirs was the only unspoiled world he'd ever encountered."[7] O'Doyle's introduction to the Eichers paints them as a vulnerable unit, "unspoiled," but in need of protection, a side of her family Annabel would not have been able to fully understand or articulate.

The point of view continues to shift several more times throughout the first half of the novel. We have moments of close third person narration from Asta, during which she reveals her relationship with Cornelius Pierson. On Christmas, after receiving flowers from Cornelius, Asta reflects on the companionship she found from Pierson's letters: "She knows certain passages of his letters by heart. From the beginning, he has addressed the gulf between them, the loneliness that led them to correspond, his desire to marry, his standards and means."[8] A major factor of the loneliness Asta references was the death of her husband, Heinrich, and the strained, and often abusive, relationship the couple had before his death.

The varied points of view allow us to feel as though we completely know the family and their lives leading up to the murders. Phillips invents their interiority, even the details of Asta's sex life, to make her characters real. Though they did

6 Ibid., 13.
7 Ibid., 17.
8 Ibid., 46.

once exist in reality, it would be impossible for us, completely removed from the Eichers in time, to know them as anything more than victims in a historical crime.

Phillips's approach to dramatization and invention is also notable in the way she handles the details of the actual crime. In the real-life 1931 trial, Harry Powers (real name Harm Drenth), was indicted for murder and executed by the state of West Virginia. The evidence against him was damning, but circumstantial. There was no record in existence of what actually happened during the murder of Asta and her children, and Powers didn't offer a detailed confession. Like many of the details that are impossible to know about the event, Phillips could have invented the details of the murder on her own and presented them as truth in narrative, but she does not. She

By creating this scene in Emily's mind, Phillips allows us to experience the cruelty and rage that Powers felt during the murders...

could have given Harry Powers a section from his point of view, detailing through his own eyes what he did to Asta, Hart, Grethe, and Annabel, but she does not do that either. Instead, the only accounts of the murders, other than the circumstantial evidence presented at trial, appear in the imagination of the characters, particularly through Emily Thornhill's visions, dreams, and suppositions, and the after-life observations of the deceased Annabel.

Emily Thornhill covers the Powers case as a reporter for the *Chicago Tribune*. She feels such a powerful attraction to the Eicher family and to the details of the case that she adopts the family's orphaned dog and carries around discarded drawings of Annabel Eicher's. During her reporting, Emily learns disturbing facts about the murders. During the initial investigation, the sheriff tells her that the female victims were not "sexually attacked," but Hart Eicher had been "emasculated."[9] It was also revealed that Dorothy Lemke, one of Powers's other victims, was bald when they found her body, and that the cause for her hair loss could have been "severe fright or trauma." These details cause Emily to recreate the crime scene in her imagination as well as in her dreams. While thinking of Lemke, Emily says she "would never tell it, never write it, for there was no way to prove it, but she knew what Powers had said and done. Bound, Dorothy broke the noose and dropped to the basement floor. Roused to fury, Powers showed her his secret."[10] This indicates that Powers had shown Hart's severed penis to Dorothy Lemke to taunt and frighten her before he killed her. As Emily admits, there is no way to prove this. There is no court document or record that indicates these events happened. By creating this scene in Emily's mind, Phillips allows us to experience the cruelty and rage that Powers felt during the murders, as well as the fear and disgust of his victims.

Annabel also offers important details of the crime. After her death, Annabel becomes a narrator from the afterlife. In an interview with NPR, Phillips claims that Annabel's after-life narration is not the result of her being a ghost. "She doesn't appear to anyone," she says. "She can turn in the breath of a thought, she can move in and out of time. She sees things that may be, or things that will be, so it's more almost a physics problem, you know. Where does all this energy go, especially in the case of very sudden deaths?"[11] This particular physics problem helps Phillips create and relay more of the missing details of Powers's crime. Annabel's spirit sees her beloved doll, Mrs. Pomeroy, in the mud at the murder scene. She places the doll in Powers's car and then "tells Emily" through a dream.[12]

This piece of evidence helps investigators place the Eicher children with Powers during the last day of their lives.

Other than Emily's brief imaginings and Annabel's ghostly glimpses of the murder scene, the actual event of the murder is essentially left out. It is the one part of the story left to the reader's imagination. It is interesting that Phillips takes great liberties in the creation of internal lives for the characters, but left out what would seem to be the most important information. In the interview that accompanies the novel, Phillips says her intent with this book was to "make the victims real and their lives meaningful, to capture moving, quiet moments in their experience that would make them unforgettable. I could only do this through transforming the story in my imagination as fiction."[13] A simple reporting that the crimes occurred would lack the strong emotions Phillips is able to create through the imagined details of the crime and of the Eichers' lives preceding the crime.

Another effective approach Phillips uses in her repurposing of the Eicher murders is the use of artifacts woven throughout the story. Phillips inserts photographs, letters, and newspaper articles throughout the narrative. On page eighty-five we see a letter from Cornelius (Harry Powers) to Asta's daughter, Grethe. On 159 is a series of excerpts from newspaper articles and telegrams, followed with grainy black and white photographs of the Eicher family on page 161. In the acknowledgements, Phillips asserts that these artifacts are real

9 Ibid., 184.

10 Ibid., 192.

11 Lynn Neary. "*Quiet Dell* Revives a Depression-Era Murder Story," NPR, 15 October 2013, accessed 17 March 2016, http://www.npr.org/2013/10/15/234681427/quiet-dell-revives-a-depression-era-murder-story

12 Phillips, *Quiet Dell*, 238.

13 Ibid., 456.

and true to the original 1930s reportage of the crime. I recently corresponded with Phillips via email and asked her why she chose to duplicate real news footage and photographs when so much of the novel is fictionalized. In her response, Phillips stated, "I decided on what to include based on the fiction. That is, the reality of the story was meant to back up the novel, with the invented story becoming the world for the reader, and the photos/newspaper quotes, and quotes from literature, coming in between sections, to remind the reader that there is a 'real story' behind the fiction." She continues by saying that in the novel, "reality is used to underscore the world of the fiction."[14] By dramatizing the events, Phillips repurposes the memory of a sensationalized murder into a tribute to the victims that reminds readers that, once, the Eichers were more than simply names in a headline.

Phillips's use of dramatization and artifacts are only a couple of methods a writer could use to repurpose a true event in fiction. In examining approaches, it is important to look at the event itself. Can any real life event be repurposed into fiction? Many writers may tell you that certain occurrences in their fiction really happened. They rob the cradle, to employ one of the techniques Gwyn Hyman Rubio suggested to give them ideas—a character breaks his arm in a novel because in the author's childhood he'd suffered a broken arm and has vivid memories of the pain of recovery, or a fictional father doles out the same type of punishment the author's own father used while he was a child. This is repurposing on a smaller scale. Small events may be repurposed into other small, fictional events. But what makes a big event, one worthy of an entire novel, repurposeable?

I believe there are specific criteria that make a major event eligible for successful repurposing. First, the event must be able to withstand space and time. A sensationalized murder, for example, is an event that could resonate with readers regardless of time period or location. In an interview, the Irish novelist Colum McCann stated, "I think that if someone looks back in fifty years at what writers are doing today, they will see that we're taking these real people and creating fiction around them."[15] When writers write fiction about historical people and events, the aim is to focus on the truth of the human condition and the humanity behind events, which is universal regardless of location and time.

Secondly, to be repurposeable in fiction, an event must have a haunting quality. In an *Appalachian Heritage* interview, novelist Lee Smith says ideas for novels often start with an image, and "won't disappear with the raves of time." She says she was going to write her novel *Guests on Earth*, which repurposes the historical events, in the late 1980s, though it took her many years to actually begin. She says, "just the very fact that it won't go away means to me that this is something that's somehow really important and I need to pursue it."[16] Events that haunt us through memory or through fascination with research become prime material for repurposing.

Finally, and what I find most important in my own work, the question of whether or not an event can be successfully repurposed is one of ownership. Whose story is this? The successfully repurposed story belongs to the community. The events that occur in these stories transcend ownership. The consequences of the event ripple throughout a community and have implications in the lives of many, and to be successful in the repurposing, the fiction that results from it must indicate

14 Jayne Anne Phillips, Email interview with the author, 16 March 2016.

15 John Cusatis. *Understanding Colum McCann* (Columbia: University of South Carolina Press, 2011), 175.

16 Jason Howard. "An *Appalachian Heritage* Interview with Lee Smith." *Appalachian Heritage* 42, no. 1 (Winter 2014): 54, 55.

that communal aspect. In "Concerning Quiet Dell," Jayne Anne Phillips says she had been fascinated by the Eicher murders since childhood. She says, "My mother used to tell me that she remembered holding her mother's hand, walking along a crowded dirt road in the heat and dust of August—cars parked on either side as far as she could see—past a 'murder garage' being taken apart, piece-by-piece, by souvenir-seekers. She was six years old."[17] Just as I have vivid memories of watching the O.J. Simpson and Susan Smith murder trials with my family on television, Phillips's mother had memories of learning about the conviction and execution of Harry Powers, and she passed those down to Phillips. Such large and public events leave their mark on all members of a community.

It is important to remember that repurposing a historical event requires more than simply inserting factual details into fiction. The event must be made into something new, given a new purpose. In "Raiding the Larder: Research in Fact-Based Fiction," Debra Spark says, "when it comes to fiction, information is only interesting because it is part of the story, because it has an emotional or narrative reason for being."[18] We can only rob from the headlines successfully when we use historical events in meaningful ways that give fresh purpose to the details and the emotional truth of the history. ■

17 Phillips, "Concerning *Quiet Dell*."

18 Debra Spark. "Raiding the Larder: Research in Fact-Based Fiction," *The Writer's Chronicle*, September 2014, accessed 20 March 2016, https://www.awpwriter.org/magazine_media/writers_chronicle_view/3513/raiding_the_larder_research_in_fact-based_fiction

BEULAH

She's sitting in a straight chair,
romance book open,
coffee cold with rainbows,
alone most of the time
with oxygen tank's tubes and masks,
baskets of prescription pill bottles.

With company, she is in her element,
cooking, walking
as far as the cord can reach.
She gives the lot of us advice on winning
in business, in love.
She can tell you the best way to handle a divorce,
get a baby to sleep or school an ex in a settlement.

"You know what your problem is..."

Her voice rasps years of cigarette smoke
a husky note in every sentence,
we winced, but now we miss her advice, her wisdom
as she cataloged where each of us went wrong
a litany of our "problems" handed out like dinner rolls.

SYLVIA WOODS

ON THE TENTH ANNIVERSARY OF JAMES STILL'S PASSING

This last day of April
we gather to celebrate and remember.
Cutworms free fall;
we laugh, slap them away,
fat green bodies that wiggle
and slide their silky curves
on our warm backs.

How they cling, hang
all their hundred legs
in this holy shrine,
where we have sung and swarped
in summers, where ballads
of lost love and old time
religion brought sweet
communion, where we wove words
like filaments on dewy spider webs
suspended over Troublesome Creek.

Were he present,
and who's to say he is not,
I reckon the old man
would chuckle at plentiful larvae
of these night flying moths. Mayhap
he would say
who he wants with him in heaven,
recite verses about butterflies on Wolfpen,

minnows that leap in
shallow pools,
happy as we to be
in these hills and of these hills,
still.

SYLVIA WOODS

JUNEBUG

CHELYEN DAVIS

From the kitchen window I can see two little girls lying in my yard like small sacks of brightly-dressed potatoes. My daughter June is walking among them, followed by another girl struggling with my wheelbarrow. June is draping one prone girl with a sheet, my good sheets, given to us by Daniel's mother when we married, the ones June's been told not to touch. The ones I don't touch either.

"We're playing 'Black Plague,'" June explains to me when I go outside, as if it should be obvious. "Hailey has died, so I have to cover her with a sheet and then we put her in the wheelbarrow and dump her by the fence because we don't have time to bury her before Madison dies. In the plague everyone died at the same time."

Madison, still lying in her spot on the ground, blinks up at me like an owl. She and Hailey and Anna—pushing the wheelbarrow—have large black circles drawn all over their neck and arms, and I'm betting that is permanent magic marker, and I don't know how to get it off and I should catch hell from their mothers.

"I didn't know how to make real boils," June says.

I should catch hell, but I won't. Their mothers won't say a word because it's only been three months since Daniel died, and so they'll look at their spotted, markered children and shake their heads. "Poor woman," they'll think. And they won't say a word, not to me, but they'll call each other. They'll let their daughters play with Poor June, and when they come to pick them up they'll ask how I'm doing but they only want me to say I'm holding up. And they'll go back to their living husbands and thank God that it wasn't them whose husband drove into a truck on a curvy road.

"Bless her heart, how awful for her, I thought I might take her a casserole," they say. "How lucky we are," they think. As if Dead Husband is catching.

Today it's the Black Plague. Before that it was death by volcano. It's that History Channel Daniel let her watch. We should have never gotten the satellite dish.

"Did you know about Herculaneum?" June asked. "It was beside Pompeii. Pompeii got covered by a volcano, and it's in all the books, but Herculaneum was right next door and it had a thermal blast. That means the air was 900 degrees, and it hit the people, and it boils your brains and vaporizes your skin and you die in a second, because it's so hot." June is excited by this. "I would think that having your brain boiled would hurt, even for that tiny little second, and that if your skin would vaporize so would your eyeballs, probably, and that would hurt too. They say it would only take you less than a second to die, but surely you'd feel it, wouldn't you? Wouldn't you know? Even for that split-second? How hot is our oven?"

She waited a moment, and looked at me, and I could see that Daniel would have said, "That's really cool," or maybe even "Let's go look at the oven and see," and I had failed a test here. I was supposed to be excited, to join in the game, speculate on how long it takes to die, suggest we go to the Internet and look up more information together.

She wants to talk about horrible ways to die and I can see this is something psychological and that it's about Daniel but I just cannot deal with it.

Daniel didn't get beheaded, or die of a plague, or have his brains boiled by volcanic air. It was nothing exciting at all. He drove into a truck...

Lord only knows. Daniel let her read grownup books, watch all kinds of TV, and showed her stuff on the Internet. I tried to steer her toward cartoons and girly shows but it was two to one. Daniel and June in their own little world of science and history and God knows what. And now he's gone and I'm left with her and all the weird stuff stored up in her brain and cached in our browser.

Daniel didn't get beheaded, or die of a plague, or have his brains boiled by volcanic air. It was nothing exciting at all. He drove into a truck—twisty mountain roads, poor line of sight, so sad but so ordinary. He was probably thinking of something like whether our house is really riddled with miniscule parasites like the news said. He'd have been disappointed his own death was so boring.

He was always that way, wondering how the world worked, a tinkerer. "Airy-fairy," my mother said, his head in the clouds, but she liked him even so. I brought him home from college and his favorite part of the visit was when I showed him how to tie a string to the leg of a junebug and watch it fly in circles over your head. You've got to tie the knot at the knee, if that's what it is, just right or the leg will come off. It'll come off eventually anyway, and the junebug will fly away free and its leg will grow back. That fascinated Daniel. "I wish we could regenerate like that," he said. That's how we named June.

I know that what June really wants to know is how does it feel to be hit by a truck? How long does it take to die afterwards? Did her dad lie in the road, looking at the sky and wondering who would come tell us? I won't tell her that Daniel was lucky if he was killed instantly.

I only once saw June cry over Daniel. When I told her he was gone she threw the biggest fit you ever saw. She was a wild thing, clawing and screaming and calling me a liar. She cried herself to sleep, and then it was over. She never said another word about him. She just got obsessed with violent death.

So I'm trying to keep an eye on June. I told her the oven won't go even halfway to 900 degrees, and that if I catch her near it I'll show her what a slow and painful death is really like. And then I cried, because it reminded me of Daniel, and I could see in her face that it reminded her too, and I try to remember she's a little girl who lost her daddy, not some stranger bound to blow us both up with an ill-advised experiment.

Yet. Today. Today we're not blowing us both up. Today it's plague and thermal blasts. I don't know what tomorrow is. With June tomorrow might be tsunamis or Viking raids or waterboarding, for God's sake Daniel let her watch CNN so who knows. I had better hide the garden hose.

I know what it will not be. It will not be pink dresses and Barbie dolls (unless they get beheaded, or boiled, or locked in a tower) or ponies or teddy bears or any of the little-girl stuff that I had, that I understand. When we found out she was coming that's what I thought I was getting, a little me, and my mother and I decorated the baby's room in pink paper and yellow ducks. Daniel laughed and said it clashed but he didn't care, he was over the moon about her since the first time we went to the doctor and heard her heartbeat. "I wish we could record this and let her hear it later," he said. Little did he know then but she'd have loved that. "Listen to the blood," she'd have said.

I carried her in my belly for nine months and I gave up wine for her and I nursed her and I changed her diapers, but she still reached for Daniel first. I bought her first dolls but when she could choose she wanted a stuffed dinosaur. And then it couldn't stay in the same toybox as her dolls because "dinosaurs and humans didn't live at the same time, Mommy."

It was summer when Daniel died and the grief felt strange, almost inappropriate in the season of heat and life and pool parties and barbecues. It seemed wrong to think about death and about sunscreen at the same time. Now it's October and finally the grief feels more comfortable, like it fits better. Now everything's dying, everyone's mourning, I don't stand out as much. It's like I put on a heavy winter coat before everyone else and it took this long for it to be the right season for it.

Fall has always made me think of the past, of dead times. My childhood was the seventies, preserved forever in the amber of earth-toned Polaroids, in which everything had a brownish, warm-looking tint to it. Harvest Gold in the leaves and on our Fridgidaire, peeking out from behind my drawings stuck on with alphabet magnets.

Out in the present fall, Hailey has been disposed of, sitting quietly by the fence with my good sheet trailing into the onion grass, and Madison is in the wheelbarrow. June is pointing at something bossily. Perhaps she's lecturing on how it really felt to die of the plague. Maybe the other girls aren't suffering realistically enough.

I wish I could fly away like a junebug, I'd sacrifice a leg for it, for the freedom to not be here for a while, not be always all wrapped up in missing Daniel and worrying about June. Missing, worrying, missing, worrying, circling around my head like a bug on a string. I wish I could regenerate what's missing.

I hear car engines and doors closing. The mothers are here to fetch their daughters. I'll see their eyebrows fly up at sight of magic-marker boils, before they're wrestled back down into a neutral expression. They'll pack up their daughters and give me fake hugs and go, because they don't know what to say to me. And June and I will stay here, looking at each other, strangers alone together. ■

HE TELLS HER A LOVE POEM

This is all your fault—
Every bit of it.
When we came here for the first time,
You said, "I want my house right there."
Like I could wave my hand
Turn bull thistle, broom sedge,
Joe Pye and Goldenrod into
Orchard grass and flowers,
Turn a wilderness into a retreat,
A little beaten path into a doorway.
But no use whining:
So I set to doing it.
A house, barn, ponds,
Sheds, gates, wells dug,
Eight miles of fence,
Cedars cut and piled to the sky
Buckets of sweat later,
Fifteen years of it,
And I still look over at you
Sitting on the porch
Smiling at the ridgeline
Your pretty hands cradling your cup
And the rush of feeling
Fills my eyes, catches in my throat.
I can read all kinds of sign
Know the smell of weather
The ways of everything living
But you are the mystery
I can't solve.
You are the why
In every sore muscle and bloody blister

The root of every tangle
Every strike of the ax
Every shovel full of dirt
Turned in search of the key
To your heart's puzzle.

RITA QUILLEN

WHEN THE CHILDREN COME HOME

When the children come home
We don't kill the fatted calf
But we do cook both ham and turkey
Casseroles and pies and fruit and flowers
Table groaning under the sacrament
Borne of blood and absence,
Every visit prodigal in its intensity
But not really:
Because they aren't staying.
When the children come home
And then leave again
We look at the acres cleared inch by inch,
Dollar by dollar,
The fence built foot by sweaty, bleeding foot
Wonder why in the world
Why
In the world we have spent
The one tiny spark from a campfire
That is our time here
On such a fool's errand.
On giving them something they need
Like a rotary telephone or a wringer washer
Imagine strangers wondering through
Saying, "How much?"
Fields taken back by wild rose
And bull thistle
The auctioneer's gavel
Sounding a death knell
Words of such love

Such longing choke in our throats
A cry or a sigh
Never told until that final day
After all is said and done and over
When the children come home.

RITA QUILLEN

BOOK REVIEW

Lee Smith. *Dimestore: A Writer's Life*. Chapel Hill, N.C..: Algonquin Books of Chapel Hill, 2016. 202 pages. Hardcover. $24.95.

Reviewed by Amy D. Clark

Dimestore: A Writer's Life is a collection of fifteen essays, published over the span of twenty years. "This little book," as Lee Smith called it in a recent reading in Abingdon, Virginia, is thematically anchored—as the title suggests—in the places to which Smith credits her early training as a writer. Loyal readers will recognize her descriptions of narratives built around the lives of the dolls her father sold in his store, as well as her observations of patrons from high up in the office window. As a child she watched as they shopped—and shoplifted. "Thus," she says, "I

learned the position of the omniscient narrator, who sees and records everything, yet is never visible. It was the perfect early education for a fiction writer."

Zoom out to her hometown of Grundy, Virginia, which Smith recalls as "filled with our relatives" who owned or ran many of the businesses, the schools, and the theatre where she learned that "place can be almost as important as personality." It is the sense of place that she returns again and again in this collection, just as she does in her novels.

Many of Smith's readers will relate as she discusses the complicated intersection between old and new, a common theme in Appalachian literature. For Smith, it begins with the dichotomy of past and present in her hometown. Dividing the two is the Levisa river, described as "tame" enough for a group of little girls to float downriver on homemade rafts, but a "raging torrent" when it destroyed homes, businesses, and lives. The river seems an apt metaphor as Smith journeys through her memories; indeed, "Big River" recounts her literal trip down the Mississippi with fifteen Hollins classmates, a trip which inspired the novel *The Last Girls*. "Suddenly," she writes, "I had plenty of conflict brought to us by the simple passage of life itself."

The early essays include conflicts as divorce, uncertainty, and a pattern of mental illness in her family, which Smith discusses with raw honesty. Both of her parents suffered from conditions that required hospitalizations, as described in the essay "Kindly Nervous," the favored family euphemism for the conditions. She writes tenderly about her late son Josh, who suffered from psychotic episodes, in "Goodbye to the Sunset Man," perhaps the most deeply personal of the pieces. She shows us the unpredictability of life with a disabled child, and the agony of losing him. But herein we see the healing power of water, as Smith concludes the essay with the scattering of his ashes from a schooner in Key West. She ushers readers through "A Life in Books," where she reveals the "oceanic" wake of grief and rage left by her son's death. Her doctor's prescription: write every day. The result was the novel *On Agate Hill.*

Smith also describes learning to transition from writing what she knew (the mantra of writing workshops) to writing what she learned in her careers as a journalist and teacher. "I write fiction," she muses, "the way other people write in their journals." She compares the act of writing to an "addiction," a "physical joy," a feeling that is "almost sexual." She refers to her writing self as a "conduit" and a "stenographer," who captures the narratives that arrive in "a human voice...somewhere deep inside me."

Smith closes the book where she begins: her childhood home that she describes with such color and gaiety. But the memories for her are bittersweet. "It's like those awful claws beneath the festive table at my grandmother's house," she writes in "Angels Passing." Her family grappled with their problems, as do all families. "In the parlance of today, our family was dysfunctional," she admits, before asking, "(Is any family not?)"

Each of the essays examines the scope of her writing life as she negotiates her roles as daughter, wife, mother ... and author. Smith reminds us that in life, as in her novels, there is neither a tidy plot nor ending. "Certainly, the linear, beginning-middle-end form doesn't fit the lives of any women I know," she says. "For life has turned out to be wild and various, full of the unexpected, and it's a monstrous big river out here."

Though Smith says she does not consider herself an autobiographical writer, these pieces are rendered in a familiar voice, one that sounds so much like those of the protagonists her readers cherish. Whether readers are aspiring authors or loyal followers of her work, *Dimestore* is a treasure trove of anecdotes and advice, of memory and loss, of humor and love. ■

CANTICLE OF SUMMER

O furnace
bless the blast

eneagon weld
beyond
your angles

& staves of
rib cage
bless the lungs

& the blood
& the red bless

the yellow
you become

Face bless this sun
& all the rays
of its relation

rays bless your reach
& ground bless
the street

palm bless the kiss
& the ease
some have
to please

Blow bless the breeze
& fear bless
the wind

that bends
& lifts
the trees

branches
bless the sap
& sap bless

the green
that burns
from blast
to floating ash

O grief bless
the hours raking
now into the past

ELIZABETH SAVAGE

CONTRIBUTORS

Samantha Atkins is a fiction writer from southern Indiana working on her MFA at Purdue University. She is the coordinator of Purdue's visiting writers series and also the nonfiction editor of *Sycamore Review*. Atkins's work can be found in *Tahoma Review* and the Madrid-based bilingual magazine *Humanize*. She was also short-listed for *Glimmer Train*'s New Writer Award in May 2015.

A finalist for the 2015 James Wright Poetry Award, **Lana Austin**'s work has appeared in *Mid-American Review, The Writer's Chronicle, Southern Women's Review,* and *Zone 3*. Her first chapbook, *In Search of the Wild Dulcimer,* is forthcoming from Finishing Line Press. Austin has an MFA from George Mason University. Born and raised in Kentucky, she has lived in England and Italy but currently resides in Alabama with her husband and three children.

Amy Clark's writing has appeared or is forthcoming in *The New York Times, Salon, NPR, Still, Appalachian Heritage, Blue Ridge Country, Appalachian Journal,* and many others. Her co-edited book, *Talking Appalachian: Voice, Identity, and Community,* was used as a dialect resource for actors during the filming of *Big Stone Gap,* a movie adaptation of Adriana Trigiani's novel of the same title.

Chelyen Davis formerly worked as a journalist for several Virginia newspapers. Her fiction work has previously appeared in *Appalachian Heritage* and in the *Still: The Journal* 2014 Fiction Writing Contest. Her essays on aspects of Appalachian culture have appeared in several media outlets. A native of southwest Virginia, she currently lives in Richmond.

Chapman Hood Frazier is a Professor in Residence for James Madison University and was a poetry editor for *The Dos Passos Review* and guest-editor for the *Hampden Sydney Poetry Review.* He has published poetry in a variety of publications including *The Virginia Quarterly Review, The South Carolina Review,* and *Appalachian Heritage,* and is currently working on a collection of interviews with contemporary poets.

Jesse Graves is the author of two collections of poetry, *Tennessee Landscape with Blighted Pine* and *Basin Ghosts*. He is co-editor of three volumes of ***The Southern Poetry Anthology*** and of the forthcoming *Complete Poems of James Agee*. His poems have appeared in recent or forthcoming issues of *Prairie Schooner, Blackbird, Carolina Quarterly*, and ***The Missouri Review***. Graves is an associate professor of English at East Tennessee State University.

A native of upper East Tennessee, **Jane Hicks** is an award-winning poet and quilter. Her poetry appears widely in journals and anthologies. Her "literary quilts" illustrate the works of playwright Jo Carson and novelists Sharyn McCrumb and Silas House and were featured in *Blue Ridge Country Magazine*. Hicks has published two poetry collections, *Blood and Bone Remember* (2005) and *Driving with the Dead* (2014).

Silas House is the nationally bestselling author of six novels, most recently *Same Sun Here* (with Neela Vaswani), as well as three plays and one book of creative nonfiction. He is a frequent contributor to the *New York Times* and his writing has appeared in *Newsday, Oxford American, Narrative*, and many others. House serves as the NEH Chair of Appalachian Studies at Berea College and on the fiction faculty at Spalding University's MFA in creative writing.

Christopher McCurry is an editor at Accents Publishing and a high school English teacher. His poetry has appeared in ***Diode, The Louisville Review, The Los Angeles Review, Rattle***, and others. In 2013 Holly Goddard Jones selected his short story for ***Still: The Journal***'s fiction prize. His second chapbook, *Nearly Perfect Photograph*, was published earlier this year. He is the co-founder of *Workhorse* and lives in Lexington, Kentucky, with his wife and daughter.

Laura Leigh Morris lives in Greenville, South Carolina, where she is an Assistant Professor at Furman University. She has previously published short fiction in ***The Louisville Review, Weave Magazine***, *Conclave: A Journal of Character*, and other journals. "Muddin'" is part of her collection, *Jaws of Life and Other Stories*, a book currently in search of a publisher.

Beth Newberry is a writer and editor living in Louisville, Kentucky. Her work has been published in *Sojourners, Still: The Journal*, and *The Louisville Review*. Her essay "The Center of the Compass" was named a notable essay of 2010 by Robert Atwan in the 2011 *Best American Essays*. She writes at thehillville.com.

Christopher Petrucelli is a graduate student at the University of Alaska, Fairbanks and an associate poetry editor at *Stirring a Literary collection*. His poetry has appeared in *Connotation Press, Rappahannock Review, Still: The Journal*, and elsewhere. His chapbook, *Action at a Distance*, is available from UIndy's Etchings Press.

Rita Quillen's latest poetry collection, *The Mad Farmer's Wife*, is forthcoming in fall 2016 from Texas Review Press. Quillen is the author of the novel *Hiding Ezra*, the chapbook *Something Solid To Anchor To*, the poetry collections *Her Secret Dream, October Dusk*, and *Counting the Sums*, and an essay collection *Looking for Native Ground: Contemporary Appalachian Poetry*. She lives and farms on Early Autumn Farm in Scott County, Virginia.

Amanda Jo Runyon is a mother, writer, and instructor in Pike County, Kentucky. Her fiction and poetry have appeared in journals such as *The Louisville Review, Still: The Journal, Pine Mountain Sand and Gravel*, and *Kudzu*, as well as *Seeking Its Own Level*, volume 4 of the *Motif* anthology series. She is co-editor of the literary journal *The Pikeville Review*.

Elizabeth Savage is professor of English at Fairmont State University and poetry editor for *Kestrel: A Journal of Literature & Art*. She is author of *Idylliad* (2015) and *Grammar* (2012), both from Furniture Press. Dancing Girl Press has just published a new chapbook, *Parallax*.

Vic Sizemore's writing has appeared in or is forthcoming in *StoryQuarterly, Southern Humanities Review, Portland Review, storySouth, Connecticut Review, Blue Mesa Review, Sou'wester, Reed Magazine*, and elsewhere. "It Was Dead When I Got It" is part of his essay collection *Get Thee Behind Me*. His fiction has won the New Millennium Writings Award and has been nominated for the Best American Nonrequired Reading series and two Pushcart Prizes.

Sylvia Woods is a native Kentuckian and former high school English teacher in Oak Ridge, Tennessee. Her work has been published in literary journals and anthologies, including *Appalachian Heritage, Southern Poetry Anthology III: Appalachia,* and *Southern Poetry Anthology VI: Tennessee.*

John Thomas York grew up on a farm in northwestern North Carolina and now lives in Greensboro. His poetry has recently appeared in *Appalachian Journal, Kenyon Review Online, North Carolina Literary Review, Tar River Poetry,* and *Town Creek Poetry.* In 2012, Press 53 published his first full-length collection, *Cold Spring Rising.* For over thirty-seven years, he taught English in North Carolina's public schools, until his retirement in 2016.